Where I Was Young

Where I Was Young

Memories of London Childhoods

VALERIE JENKINS

With line drawings by
George Murray

Hart-Davis, MacGibbon London

Granada Publishing Limited
This collection first published in Great Britain 1976 by Hart-Davis,
MacGibbon Ltd
Frogmore, St Albans, Hertfordshire AL2 2NF and
3 Upper James Street, London W1R 4BP

Text copyright © 1973, 1974, 1976 by Beaverbrook Newspapers Limited
Illustrations copyright © 1976 by Hart-Davis, MacGibbon Limited

ISBN 0 246 10873 8

Printed in Great Britain by
Fletcher & Son Ltd, Norwich

Contents

CONTENTS

Introduction

The idea was to ask a number of people who had been brought up in London to go back to the area of the city where they spent their formative years, see how the area had altered, and generally reminisce about the lives they had lived in that place. We would look at, say, Tottenham or Belgravia through the eyes of someone who had spent impressionable years there. A childhood in one would have a distinctly different flavour from a childhood in the other. It was impossible to say which of the two would be more definitively a London childhood.

I had no fixed age group in mind, but as it turned out the age span of the subjects was half a century, from youngster John Herbert, son of A. P. H., at 50, to the remarkable Sir Charles Tennyson, grandson of Lord Alfred, who is now 97. A real Victorian, Sir Charles was able to say in passing, as we walked around Sussex Place, 'Let's see now. Ah yes, we must have left here in 1886.'

Nobody's reminiscences are ever dull; even post-war children already have a store of nostalgia. But I was struck by the fact that the older people were, the more they were full of enthusiasm and racontage. People's backgrounds have become so uniform, their culture so universal, that we have to turn to those beyond middle age for the most bizarre and eccentric memories. As Ivor Newton, at 83, commented, 'Today everyone looks like a bank clerk.'

It was a good point in the century to look back. In the 1970s we are at a lucky juncture: there are still legions of people around who remember the late Victorian and the Edwardian era; but as they get fewer the opportunity to hear at first hand what city life was like before the advent of the internal-combustion engine should be seized. For it was the motor car, coinciding with the First World War, which formed the greatest divide in

1

our century. Horsedrawn London was a dramatically different place. It is only now that we are questioning whether the alterations have been a progression or a ghastly mistake. Motor traffic has been the greatest single factor in changing the shape of the city and the hardest to imagine life without.

Despite the proliferation of conservationist groups, and the constant battle against bad city redevelopment waged all around me so strenuously by colleagues on the *Evening Standard*, I was still not quite prepared for what I was shown so sharply and graphically by my very first interviewee in the series. This happened to be Louis Heren, deputy editor of *The Times*.

We went to Dellow Street, in Shadwell, down by the docks. There, what had been in his childhood a noisy, action-filled street, where people would put their tables and chairs on the pavement outside in summer, where tradesmen came by and horses clattered along the cobbles, where housewives chatted and children played, where there were stables and pubs and a community spirit that Heren likened to that of Naples, had become an utterly lifeless scene. Dellow Street is now a passageway between towering, featureless blocks of council flats.

It was the silence that struck us as much as anything, the silence not of tranquillity but of emptiness. Not a soul walked, talked, shouted, played; not even a face peered from a window. The terraced cottages before may have been unhygienic but they formed the street into a unit looking out on to its world, and people in that street felt they could relate to it. Then the motor car came, rendering street life dangerous and unappealing, and the modern architects with designs derived from the shoe-box, and the human beings were driven indoors, behind their little locked doors. It was a story I was to hear again and again, like an old refrain.

There was no preconceived format for each interview, apart from the trip to the old homestead. Sometimes the recollections were largely interior, the house being all important; sometimes they were more emotional, so much so that the subject could not bear to step inside the house, preferring to remember it as it had been. Sometimes it was the parent relationship that obsessed; others barely mentioned their parents at all. A few dwelt on people outside their families, nannies and schoolteachers particularly, who had influenced their development. But, essentially, the intention was to evoke a special geographical area: John Betjeman's Highgate, Osbert Lancaster's Notting Hill, the Harris brothers' River Thames. (We should cling to our river guardians especially: soon there will be even fewer people who actually work on the river, or who remember it as a busy flourishing highway, laden with cargo.)

I could, I suppose, have sat down with everyone and just talked about

2

his or her childhood; but it was much more profitable actually to go back, to locate particularities and details – the old garden roller, rusting away after fifty years; the lion's head door-knocker; the very avenue of trees from the garden of a once vast mansion, which is now the line of a built-up suburban crescent.

Some people were keener to go back and take a look than others. Philip Hope-Wallace was so moved by the experience that he could not face the theatre the same evening. Dame Edith Evans was positively antipathetic to the whole idea: 'Hate going back. Can't remember anything. All a hundred years ago.' Others were so full of memories they had already written whole books of their own on the subject.

It is almost impossible to generalize about any group of people. But I was struck by what is probably a cliché – that what are misnamed deprived backgrounds produce the most dramatic and vivid memories, and are often the more fondly recalled for that. Who cared about a few bugs and nine-to-a-bed when every day there might quite accidentally be scenes of bloodshed and fury, mirth and circus antics, the natural order in the poverty-stricken home? I don't think any cosy middle-class home could match the daily thrills and disasters in the lives of the Chegwidden family of Poplar; no Kensington home that I came across boasted a mother who killed the cat by suffocation during an epileptic fit, as happened *chez* the Dolly Sisters in the East End.

It isn't that the aristocratic tales were not also exciting: I loved to hear first-hand accounts of Tennyson and Swinburne (kissing infants' heads again), Queen Victoria (passing by and smiling directly at one interviewee), Lady Ottoline Morrell, William Morris, Augustus John, George Bernard Shaw, Lytton Strachey, V. Sackville West, Lord Kitchener, Sarah Siddons, Sir John Millais, Edward Elgar – all swept through the distant memories of interviewees, dropping an ironic aphorism here and there. I valued them enormously; but I think I laughed even more uproariously with the Cheg-widdens and their like, who unknown to the world at large managed to create their own home theatre. For great names do not, or did not then, sweep down the Mile End Road.

Jack Dash's childhood friend Charlie and his trick with his glass eye; Muriel Box's newly removed tonsils being fed to the family cat; Bob Harris falling into a stream as an infant and losing all his hair for ever; the Chegwidden family chickens having their heads bitten off by a neighbour's cat: there is a brutal element in many of the stories that, though life might be generally safer and more tolerable without it, also adds a certain colour and variety to mundane existence. Against all the sociological odds, all these people genuinely enjoyed looking back on allegedly deprived child-

3

hoods. Shortly after my series finished, Arnold Wesker wrote the text for a book of East End paintings and in it voiced the typical attitude of those who grew up in slum streets, made good, and always enjoyed going back: 'I have dreams of Stepney. Recurrent dreams: I'm making my home there again, or opening a café in Brick Lane, or just walking through the streets. Why?

'I think it's because I'm surprised, constantly pleased and surprised that I'm a product of it all . . .

'That, I suppose, is the main factor drawing me back again and again – I enjoy having a past. Of course everyone does, but some pasts are more bland than others. I know because friends have complained to me about them! Mine, ours, was vivid. Dirty, poverty-stricken, but I enjoy possessing it, being able to show it to people.'

Street games, each in their season, gave a communal vitality to working-class life, worlds away from the nanny crocodile to the Park. It is the sense of community, comradeship and neighbourliness that makes happy childhoods, not ease and comfort. I remember Dorothy Scannell (née Dolly Chegwidden) saying that as a child she had longed to be the only child of rich parents. But she could not have known how uneventful that would have been, however ordered and secure.

The middle-middle class world has, I found, altered least of all, despite its own belief that it has been hardest hit economically over these decades. The richer echelons have seen their vast and grand houses razed or developed into luxury flatlets: front doors now bear twenty-four doorbells, not one; and the Jay family's Tower House at Woolwich became, between the wars, seven or eight whole streets of suburbia. At the same time the characteristic working-class homes, in terraced cottages where everyone had their little yard and a sense of belonging, have been replaced by sanitary but faceless blocks that were, time and again, likened by former residents to a morgue, a prison, a barracks.

But the homes of the middle-middles really haven't changed all that much. Houses like the Hope-Wallaces' in Wimbledon, for instance, are characteristic of a style that has, with modifications, endured. Built around the turn of the century in the great spreading-out of London's tentacles around the railways, they accommodated then as now families with three to five children, in a manageable but fairly generous shape of home. It is perhaps the most archetypal style of English domestic architecture, solid and respectable and workable, with pleasant gardens. Too much opprobrium has been heaped on the semi.

On the writers I interviewed, two particularly twentieth-century influences became apparent. One was the public library. Several of the writers I talked to, brought up in homes where books were conspicuously absent – indeed, in the case of Kingsley Amis, where reading was positively frowned upon as an anti-social activity – depended for literary sustenance on the local library, remembered as an academic haven, a hushed, green-shaded, mahogany-panelled place filled with thrilling books. Second to the library was the English mistress: the universal figure, grey of hair and wispy of figure, dogged in her perseverance in nurturing a love of the poet Tennyson even on the stoniest ground. Do these little grey ladies still exist, I wonder? Our novelists owe them vast debts.

Looking for such intimations of later distinction in the early lives of the people I saw, I was often shown some exact geographical point where they felt the first stirrings of an influence that would direct their lives.

Douglas Jay, the Labour MP, could recall the exact place where he first asked his nanny why those children were barefoot, and it was 'beyond my nurse's power to explain'; Ivor Newton listened to the church music at St Anne's, Limehouse, and was inspired, realizing 'that there was another and richer world ahead of me', towards his future as a musician.

Certain themes recurred in most memories of those of advancing years. I was often exhorted to pause and listen to the roar of passing lorries, and told that noise was once human – 'Not jet engines and juggernauts and gears grinding, but horses and carts, muffin men's bells, newsboys with placards shouting.' I heard over and over about the muffin men and the lamplighters, Chinese laundrymen in pigtails, Italian organ-grinders, prayer leaders on Sundays, the catsmeat man, the wild rabbit man, the shellfish man, the Indian toffee-seller; milk fresh from the cow at West-minster Pier. What a carnival street life was, once. There were nights of wild festivity whose memories linger for ever, like Armistice and the Relief of Mafeking and the spectacle of Zeppelins coming down; the terrible night of mourning when Queen Victoria died. There was the great cavalcade ritual of Derby Day. And, looming large in everyone's mind, rich or poor, was always that yawning gap between masters and servants. Almost everyone I interviewed made reference to the long hours and repetitive tasks inflicted on servants.

One interviewee remembered a Lizzie Pritchard from Nettlebed, a willing, rosy-cheeked girl. 'She came from a cottage in a village, and of course she wouldn't be looking at our house and saying, what lovely Georgian architecture. She would think of the stairs and the heavy scuttles of coal she had to carry up and down.' And the blackleading and hearth-stoning and the polishing of silver. But even if, now, those days are re-called as barbarous, it was still a joy to be welcomed down to the Servants' Hall to take part in wicked card-playing or be given forbidden sweets.

Occasionally a single tale or observation would call up a whole vanished era. Not just the acceptance of abundant child-bearing (Sam Oddy's grand-mother bearing seventeen children, sixteen boys and one girl) and the omnipresence of death (entire families of brothers wiped out in the First World War), but examples of things said which belong utterly to their time. Like Philip Hope-Wallace's father, speaking of a lady member of his Shakespeare reading group who aspired to a larger role: 'Who does she think she is? She's only a builder's daughter!' Or Monica Dickens's mother, driving off on her honeymoon with her bridegroom, son of the novelist, and asking him, '*Now* will you tell me what Oscar Wilde did?'

It is hard to write about London without falling back on clichés. Any-one trying to express her variety seems to get tangled up in grandiose Latinate phrases. Even David Piper, whose *Companion Guide to London* I found so useful, begins with a quotation from H. G. Wells that sums up all the pitfalls of magnumlocution: 'London is the most interesting, beautiful and wonderful city in the world to me, delicate in her incidental and multi-tudinous littleness, and stupendous in her pregnant totality . . .' Most guides at some point fall into a heap of astonished marvelling, and get buried under their own verbiage. But most of my interviewees found some way of declaring their sense of belonging to and being moulded by the city. The late Baroness Stocks wrote that her love for London must last from the dawn of life until death, and she gave her love most palpably in protecting Kensington from careless redevelopment. She also introduced me to what has become a favourite and most useful word: banausic. It means philistine, ugly, illiberal – and it describes perfectly much of Lon-don's less imaginative modern architecture.

And, of course, a writer like V. S. Pritchett is able to celebrate London in his work. He not only catches the spirit and nuances of London conver-sation in his stories, he has written the superb autobiographical volume on growing up in London, *A Cab at the Door*. In that book, he is most lyrical about the effects of exploring London in his late teens, when he was apprenticed in the Bermondsey leather trade, and felt, among those smelly streets, that he was being 'smoked and kippered' by London. That's exactly what happens to discoverers of London. Those of us who only came to London from elsewhere will never quite capture the feeling.

I should think the man who has done most to convey to us his passion-ate love of London's architecture must be Sir John Betjeman. And it was he who, some weeks after our happy day tramping round *his* old haunts on Hampstead Heath, turned the tables on me by suggesting that we should take a return visit to the place where I was young – my old school in Kings-bury, NW9. Only Sir John could have exclaimed so delightedly at a quite

6

ordinary example of suburban scholastic architecture, *circa* 1931. But he suddenly made me realize what a nice building it was, after all.

I am intensely grateful for the experience of writing this series. I want to thank Charles Wintour, editor of the *Evening Standard*, who from the beginning was so interested in the subject and so encouraging; Simon Jenkins, then Features Editor, who so freely lent from his library of books about London; and the subjects of the interviews themselves, who showed me bits of London I should never otherwise have come across. For visits to the heart of the City, to the leafy lanes of Barnes, to the bowels of the Royal Academy, and the organ loft of Westminster Abbey, to unknown markets, parks, dockyards, canals and byways, to quiet oases and humming factories, my thanks to all those who showed me, with such justified pride, their London.

CHAPTER ONE

Sir John Betjeman
Highgate

'Deeply I loved thee, 31 West Hill!' wrote Sir John Betjeman, the Poet Laureate, in his autobiographical poem 'Summoned By Bells'. It is easy to see why. It is a white mid-Victorian villa on that steep and winding slope of Highgate West Hill, banked by trees. Hampstead Heath behind it, the Burdett-Coutts estate before it, and all London below.

'Wasn't I lucky?' Sir John kept saying, as he walked around his childhood haunts in a white straw boater hat. 'Look: Hampstead Heath, Parliament Hill Fields – that elmy, hilly Middlesex scenery that Keats could see, that inspired the odes to Autumn and the Grecian Urn. Wasn't I *lucky* to be a child here?'

He was. Opposite, what is now the Holly Lodge Estate was all green fields, hornbeams and red squirrels; sheep would be driven down West Hill, interrupted by the occasional new De Dion Bouton or Delaunay-Belleville being tried out on the steep slope.

At that hill's foot did London then begin, . . . The view downhill to London puts Sir John in mind of a Thomson poem he admires and he quotes: '*And the mighty city of London, hung twixt the cloud and light, Seems a long low beach, half shingle, with a few sharp rocks upright.*' A few sharp rocks upright! A premonition of the view today, Centre Point and the Post Office Tower being the most prominent sights.

The house, where so much buttered toast was consumed, so many bridge afternoons endured, and the teddy bear Archibald so fondly loved, is now spruce in the care of Mr Iain Hamilton, former *Spectator* editor and now author of a volume of poems to which Sir John wrote a preface. 'The house looked a good deal dingier in my day,' says Sir John.

> I knew we were a lesser, lower world
> Than that remote one of the carriage folk

9

Highgate Ponds: 'that elmy hilly Middlesex scenery that inspired Keats'

> Who left their cedars and brown garden walls
> In care of servants. I could also tell
> That we were slightly richer than my friends,
> The family next door: we owned a brougham
> And they would envy us our holidays.

There were the Bowmans whose children were like brothers and sisters to John, an only child. He remembers many other neighbours. 'Next door, the cottage of the chauffeur to the Suffragan Bishop of Islington. Further down, Mrs Bunney, who I saw being carried out in her coffin.

"What would Miss Emily want with a box so long and so narrow, without any locks?" – remember de la Mare?

'And in that house, Mr Lightfoot, who would walk down to Highgate Ponds every day for a bathe, with springy step and a towel round his shoulders, and then dive from the topmost board. Even to save my life I couldn't do it.'

We had to walk round Millfield Lane to the Ponds and the Heath, to find the very spot where Sir John composed his first, very bad, poem. Highgate Ponds, on a dappled sunlight afternoon, are as ever a perfect retreat; young men are peaceably fishing. 'Nobody ever caught a thing here,' says Sir John.

'What we have under our feet is LCC grass, how lovely! Our grass used to have buttercups and daisies in profusion. And now we have some of this lovely litter to remind us that we are alive today.' But the comments are light-hearted; the Heath is as protected and as lovely an open space as Sir John could wish for. 'The addition of Ken Wood absolutely transformed this part, turning it into eighteenth-century Capability Brown.

'That's why it's so important that The Architects shouldn't get in with their tower blocks, and take advantage of the generosity of our forebears. There, you see, is Blue Star House at Archway, ruining the view, and for what? People at desks with typewriters.

'This hill is a bit of a walk I'm afraid. It didn't seem anything to me then; we would slide on a tea-tray down the grass. I say, we've come to the exact place. This is it: this is the hill: this is where I sought inspiration. I would come up here with a pencil and notepad and sit under the trees, just by a long barrow where it was said Queen Boadicea was buried. It was lovely beyond words. . . .

'And what came out?' Sir John recalls his juvenile efforts. 'Hymns Ancient and Modern'.

Nowhere else in London, Sir John says, do you get such a glimpse of the peaceful Middlesex that was. We had to take a detour across West Hill into Holly Terrace, an inner sanctum sanctorum with glades of flowering elder, ivy and beech, and limes and sycamores and the most glorious houses in silent serenity.

'Isn't it paradise? It's Keats and Leigh Hunt! Untouched Georgian railings, and gas lamps straight from Stevenson's "Lamplighter". And gravel drives that disappear into unknown grandeur. This gives you the Highgate that I knew: no combustion engines!' The residents guard their privacy, for a young man with cross eyes rushed out to ask our business. Sir John explained in his courteous way that he sought the house of his old governess, Miss Cray.

Miss Cray has of course long since departed, but next door to her house there is a wonderful old lady known in the Terrace simply as Mrs Van.

She is Henrietta (Nan) van Hooydonk, widow of the painter Hubert van Hooydonk who, she tells us, resembled Paderewski and designed the Apollo Theatre; in her hallway is one of his splendid Alma-Tadema style murals painted for a ballroom in Belgrave Square.

Mrs Van and Sir John talked of former residents both knew, of Peggy Purey-Cust and of Thalia Fisher-White: 'Everyone was hyphenated, you see,' said Sir John, 'except yours truly.' But the lovely Miss Purey-Cust has never married, and neither has Miss Fisher-White, famed for her veils. 'Perhaps,' said Mrs Van, 'their beauty kept everybody away.'

I had to confess I had been sceptical about the existence of Peggy Purey-Cust.

> O Peggy Purey-Cust, how pure you were:
> My first and purest love, Miss Purey-Cust!

11

ran the lines in 'Summoned By Bells', about the girl with streaming golden hair and turned-up nose, an Admiral's daughter, who walked with nannie, and who once asked young John Betjeman to tea.

But yes, like Joan Hunter-Dunne she was real, and there is her house at 82 West Hill, far grander than the Betjemans', with lofty entrance hall and huge expanse of sunny drawing-room, looking out on to the dome of St Paul's. Miss Purey-Cust now lives in Minehead: just a few years ago Sir John met an aunt of hers in Australia. 'She gave me a photograph of Peggy and I was absolutely right about her: golden hair and a small exquisite face. She walked rather on her toes.'

A walk around the summit of Highgate's hill with Sir John is slow, deliberate, and accompanied by comments too acerbic to relate: The Architects are regularly under fire. 'I see The Architects have been here,' Sir John will say in mock awe, 'with The Very Latest Designs.'

What is to become of Witanhurst, Highgate's stately home? 'Here Lady Crosfield gave tennis parties, too grand for such as me. I expect they will build blocks in the grounds and call them Courts and Groves, and turn this Middlesex countryside into Croydon.'

But behind the celebrated old pub, The Flask, is a delightful row of humble cottages. Pots on windowsills, coal bunkers and real old-fangled washing – pinnies, vests, dusters, combinations – blowing about on the line. 'There!' cried Sir John in glee. 'So much for the *laundromats*!'

Across the village, which John Betjeman as a child considered so plain and Georgian to 'the delightful school I went to on Southwood Lane, Highgate Junior School. Quite a walk uphill every day; probably the only reason I'm still alive today.

'Here is where Mr Kelly used to shake us till we cried; and you would be held down at the foot of this slope, so that boys could take a running jump at your bottom. Ooh it was awful, a really abominable school, after my lovely happy individual kindergarten, Byron House.'

But the junior school is where he had the extraordinary chance of meeting Mr Eliot. T. S. Eliot was known simply as 'the American master', the 'one who, I was told, liked poetry'. The incipient Poet Laureate bound his childish verse into a book, inscribed The Best of Betjeman, and gave it to him.

What did the pre-Waste Land, pre-Prufrock Eliot think of them? Later, when they met 'across the port and cheese', Mr Eliot never referred to them. But at the time a boy at school called Jelly told Betjeman that Mr Eliot thought them bad. Horrid boy called Jelly.

Walking was a chief delight of childhood, accompanied by 'my dear, deaf father'. 'We did have a brougham, which father used for the factory, and then we had a Rover motor car, and our man William, William All-right, who used to drive the brougham, had to master the motor car. My father got furious because he used to say, "It won't work." And when he polished it he would hiss at it, as though it were a horse.'

The walks of father and son would take them downhill to Kentish Town Scene, in the poem, of

> 'barking dogs,
> And costers' carts and crowded grocers' shops,
> And Daniels' store, the local Selfridge's
> The Bon Marché, the Electric Palace, slums
> That thrilled me with their smells of poverty . . .'

' "Following in Father's footsteps" was the theme of all my early child-hood,' wrote Sir John. So we must revisit the old family factory, in the Pentonville Road, passing through upper Pooterland, ponderous Vic-torian Holloway, trying to imagine where Mr Pooter's Brickfield Terrace might be.

Betjeman's made furniture of great beauty, silverware, patent locks, figured rosewood boxes to be sold in Bond Street shops,

> 'The Alexandra Palace patent lock,
> The Betjemann device for hansom cabs . . .'

and most important of all, the Tantalus, on which the family fortune had been founded. They made the frame, and an uncle had a glass factory which made the decanters.

Nowadays the works are the premises of the Medici Society, publishers of the Medici prints, and makers of greeting cards. We walked in to be surrounded by Old Master cards in unfolded piles. Traces of the old firm remain: a door engraved in florid style, 'Counting House', and the parlour with its old fireplace, where there would always be biscuits in a barrel.

Once, as a child, exploring upstairs, John Betjeman discovered a dusty drawing-room, completely furnished, where great-grandfather had lived above his work, before moving up to sylvan Highbury.

As young Master John, he was heir-apparent to the works, and he would have been the fourth-generation Betjeman (earlier an 'n' had been added to the name, in the craze for all things German) to carry on the firm. He would be taken to watch the engravers and french polishers, the cabinet-makers and locksmiths, at their work, craftsmen and artists all.

> Well now, my boy, I want your solemn word
> To carry on the firm when I am gone:
> Fourth generation, John – they'll look to you.
> They're craftsmen-artists to their fingertips . . .
> Go on creating beauty!

13

But – For myself
I knew as soon as I could read and write,
That I must be a poet.

And we must all be glad that young John Betjeman was so sure of that.

CHAPTER TWO

The 'Dolly Sisters'
Shoreditch

Everybody in the theatre knows the Dolly Sisters. They are the twins, Vi and Glad Bennett, who have just retired as seamstresses for Nathans, the theatrical costumiers. In their time they have made costumes for every name in the theatre, turning their hand to everything from Jimmy Edwards's breeches to Danny La Rue's lacy fronts.

It was Dora Bryan who gave them the name of the Dolly Sisters, during the run of Hello Dolly. The last time they came across their own favourite, Dame Sybil Thorndike, she caught sight of them and exclaimed: 'I've never forgotten you two little girls!' though the twins are in their seventies.

They were born in the same block of flats where they still live: Howard Buildings in Deal Street, E1, a Victorian block of blackened brick artisans' dwellings, due for demolition. Outside and in, it remains much the same as it was when the sisters were born in 1903.

'Mother had eight girls. They kept trying for a boy but they missed out,' says Glad, who does most of the talking. 'And funnily enough every time our mother fell for a child, Mrs Hibbert, the woman downstairs, fell for a child, and Mrs Hibbert had eight sons.

'We were the only twins in the parish so we made friends with everyone and were taken everywhere. Even if we went into the Jewish shop for a ha'porth of marmalade in a saucer, we would be given more marmalade than anyone else.'

They were dressed exactly alike until they were sixteen, in clothes made by their mother. Mother, who had sung in the chorus with Marie Lloyd in music-hall, but who was a box-maker at Bethnal Green by trade, turned to dressmaking when the vicar asked her to make him a waistcoat out of an old skirt. The sisters inherited her skill, still making all their own clothes,

Howard Buildings, Deal Street: blackened brick dwellings, due for demolition

even coats, with cloth from Berwick Street market. They favour satins and shiny fabrics even by day, and will show you how each of the microscopic beads on their beaded hems and bodices is sewn painstakingly by hand.

In the streets around Howard Buildings the Truman brewery is everywhere in evidence. Just round the corner are Truman, Hanbury and Buxton Streets, all named for the brewery, and the towers and cranes and brewery buildings dominate everything, towering over the Victorian cottages that remain, the shabby prefabs, the boarded-up rows of shops with the stamp of decay, even the spruce new school buildings and modern council blocks like Stuttle House in Spital Street.

'Our block used to be entirely for brewery men and policemen,' says Vi. 'Our father was the first tenant who wasn't police or Trumans.

'He was a sugar-boiler, till one day he got scalded with sugar, all over his face and hands. Then he went to Liptons in City Road as a flour grader. He only made twenty-eight shillings a week, so we couldn't be fed as well as we should have been. One of the daughters had rickets, and Doris died at six months. And mother used to do all her own washing, two petticoats each and goodness knows how many pinafores for seven of us.'

Adjoining their buildings are Victoria and Albert Cottages, where they

16

remember Queen Mary coming to give a prize for the best garden. The man who won was eighty-four years old. In Underwood Road, round the corner, they remember another row of cottages with pretty gardens, and a Welsh dairy with its own cowshed, where they made their own butter and cheese.

These made way for a Jewish maternity home known as Mother Levy's, where the twins' mother made all the nurses' uniforms, and the twins were taken to see the first baby boy born there. It is now the Mary Hughes Clinic Centre. They showed me the block of flats at the end of the road, Hughes Mansions, which were bombed early one morning in 1941 during the Blitz.

'In the afternoon King George and the Queen came down with Princess Elizabeth and Princess Margaret, and they walked all over the rubble. I remember a little boy saying: "But they ain't got no *crahns* on," and Margaret laughing. Oh it was a lovely memory for us.'

In the bombing they also lost the church which was so important in their lives: All Saints' in Buxton Street. They were both Sunday School superintendents there, sang in the choir, and made their first spectacular costumes for church dances.

'Our father's two sisters were missionaries in Africa, that's where we get our church side from,' said Glad. 'One of them, Annie, was due to take the children of a doctor on the *Titanic*, but two days before they sailed the children caught measles, so they had to wait for the next boat out.'

All Saints' was the centre of their social life. 'It was sad when it went. The Germans must have been trying for the Mint or the Tower. The young people had just finished redecorating the church, and putting electric lighting in, and a few weeks after it reopened this happened and it was closed for good.'

Now the site of the church is just an open space, enclosed with a wall bearing graffiti: 'Arsenal are best', 'School is nuts', 'We want swings'. The vicarage is still there, a staff house for Christ Church, Spitalfields, the neighbouring Hawksmoor church a few streets away. And the church house, Hanbury Hall (the brewers again) has just been boarded up with corrugated iron along with the little shops alongside it.

Our walk around their neighbourhood was a tiny step for them. They are great walkers. The day before I visited them, they had walked to see the rates officer at Bethnal Green, and had inadvertently walked on through Bishopsgate to Ludgate Circus before they realized how far they had come.

When they left school at fourteen they went, together and inseparable as always, to work in Ellams Jubilee Catering, off Aldgate. They were just

17

crossing Alie Street one Saturday morning during a Zeppelin raid and they saw the Minories 'running with blood'.

Then they moved to a firm making fringes, tassels and fancy cords in Vallance Road; and then they went to Bermans. This, with their early passion for the theatre, seemed like a dream fulfilled.

'It was better to work in the West End. Round here you would be on piece-work, you never knew what you were earning.' So they caught the No 6 bus every day; they stayed at Bermans eighteen years, then went to the Windmill, and then to Nathans.

Apart from these daily excursions from East End to West, they have never strayed far from home. The farthest they have travelled is from London to Bournemouth. Within one year, around 1920, the twins saw all their five sisters get married and leave home. They were left at home with mother, until mother died at eighty, still with jet-black hair.

'Even when we were sixty we still had to be in at ten o'clock each night because we were living under her roof,' says Glad. 'We couldn't go anywhere without her. She was frightened of being left on her own, and she was jealous of her own children. That was a terrible thing. Oh, she didn't go quick enough.'

Both of them got engaged several times, but they say mother would never let them marry any of the young men. 'Nobody was good enough,' said Glad.

Instead they devoted their lives to the theatre. They still sigh with delight over the first show they ever saw, when an elder sister took them to the old Lyceum to see *Boy of My Heart*. 'I'll never forget that girl in the emerald green dress, stealing pearls and jewellery and putting them in her red hair,' says Vi.

They have, of course, an enormous collection of signed pictures of stars they have dressed, Betty Grable in *Belle Starr,* Ginger Rogers in *Mame*; they have a letter from Ivor Novello written the day before he died.

Their basement living-room, which was once quite barn-like, but was divided up by their father to create a bathroom (unheard of in their childhood days), is full of pictures – not of the theatrical stars they have worked with, but of cats. Cat calendars and cat lamps that light up when plugged in, cat ornaments and even cat coasters.

'Yes, we love pussy cats,' they say. But they haven't got a cat? 'No. Mother killed him,' they told me. 'She had one of her epileptic fits and fell on him and suffocated him. She vowed she'd never have another one.'

They have become familiar figures at first nights, sitting in the front row in the gladdest of their very glad rags, their guipure lace-trimmed satins and furs, their white hair like candy floss piled high. All their money has always been spent on their theatre tickets.

'We used to get our pensions on a Thursday and spend it on a Thursday. Well, we thought we might as well enjoy ourselves before we go.' They used to go to *The Sound Of Music* on stage three times a week. They spent £350 on tickets for John Hanson in *The Desert Song*, thirty shillings a time then for seats A20 and A21 in the stalls; Saturday matinées.

They used to go to Danny La Rue twice a week; he sent them tickets and they made him cummerbunds and jabots, a fair system of barter.

'One thing we won't go to see. And that's these shows where they have a whole load of sex. Cor, blow it, if they can't behave themselves . . .' But they went to see *Oh! Calcutta!* three times? 'Yes. And the only part we did not like was when they start strapping each other up. We're broadminded, but really. Keep the party clean, we always say.'

They tell me that when they saw *Fortune And Men's Eyes* it was the first time they had ever seen a naked man.

'When we came out, the box-office manager said to us, "Did you get a good view?" and we said, "Oh, we didn't bother to look." '

CHAPTER THREE

Elisabeth Lutyens
Bloomsbury

When families still lived in Bloomsbury and the houses in the Georgian squares were homes, not offices, the composer Elisabeth Lutyens was born.

She was the fourth child of a famous father, the architect Sir Edwin Lutyens, and an aristocratic mother, Lady Emily Lytton. At three weeks old she screamed so loudly she frightened away burglars one night at the house in Bloomsbury Square. 'But for her,' wrote her mother in her diary, 'we should have lost all our silver.'

Miss Lutyens says Bloomsbury was never quite proper, socially. 'People always said, "uh, Bloomsbury", with a sneer in the voice.' But it was wonderfully central. Miss Lutyens considers her present home, a Betjeman-Victorian house in Primrose Hill, to be out in the suburbs by comparison.

We went in search of the homes of her childhood: in Bloomsbury Square, Bedford Square, and finally Mansfield Street, W1. The University of London has altered the shape of Edwardian Bloomsbury, but there are still familiar landmarks *en route*: Maitland's the chemist, and that umbrella shop on the corner of New Oxford Street, Jas Smith & Sons, 1830. 'Been there for ever,' she says. 'And I swear they are still the same umbrellas.'

Number twenty-nine Bloomsbury Square exists no more. It is the side of the square now occupied by the Liverpool Victoria Friendly Society. 'I suppose my father bought here because it was cheap. But he couldn't buy only because it was cheap: it would have to be beautiful too, or he'd be ill.'

The garden centre of the square, now an underground car park, Elisabeth Lutyens does not recall. Far more memorable is the centre of Bedford Square, where the family moved when she was eight, in 1914. 'We spent all our time playing Red Indians among the plane trees, making our faces red with geranium juices. I remember I could tie my Indian trousers tighter than any other girl in the Square. A strange ambition, which probably accounts for my chronic indigestion at present.'

The house at thirty-one Bedford Square, next to Jonathan Cape the publisher, is now the fluorescent-lit London School of Hygiene and Tropical Medicine. It is unnaturally bright, warm and lino-ed. The hallway with its pretty fanlight is the same, but it used to be lined with lead, a favourite colour of Sir Edwin Lutyens.

The room where he worked on the ground floor is now a strip-lit modern office, but the fireplace with its goddess-face moulded in plaster remains. 'A rather silly-looking woman, I always thought,' Miss Lutyens says.

Linoleum is everywhere, dismayingly: Father hated it. He would have a wooden border in Lutyens green around the Aubusson carpets.

'And all the furniture was so good it was terribly uncomfortable. Ladies sat bolt upright then, even my grandmother at ninety-five did. You never lolled.

'What I wonder,' she muses, standing in winter clothes in the blasting central heating, 'is how we ever stood the cold. There we were in our chiffon décolletages, and all we had in this vast house was a coal fire. As they say, the best way to put a fire out is to put some coal on it.'

We crept down the corridor to the back stairs, unknown territory to Miss Lutyens, who lived almost entirely on the top floor in the nursery. 'They always kept children as far away as possible. Just like *Upstairs, Downstairs* isn't it?'

The British Museum, just around the corner, was a Saturday morning haunt. 'And we had our hats made at Madame Rita, the hat shop in Museum Street.'

I asked where the four girls bought dresses. 'Oh, we had a living-in dressmaker, Miss Drake, Drakey we called her, who made all our clothes.

'They bought little lead animals in Southampton Row, called darling animals by all the family. "I'm going to get another darling animal," we'd say. And German dolls called goomies.

'I do remember the terror and excitement of the fire engines drawn by dappled grey horses that used to come up Tottenham Court Road, and the wounded soldiers in their bright blue uniforms who used to sit in the squares. We liked them, because we liked blood, horror and danger.'

The best thing about Bedford Square, she reflects, is the unchanging trees. 'Beautiful, not fussing, just blowing away for ever. London squares are unique, giving you this view. Now I've got sky on either side of me, but I do miss my trees.'

21

Mansfield Street: a royal visit to Father

But as twilight falls, the awful lighting everywhere looks utterly wrong in the graceful windows. 'Like the Nash houses in Regent's Park. Nash isn't all that good as an architect, but he's ruined by office lighting.

'Any architect worth his salt designs with light in mind, and then they go and floodlight things. Like the Shell building, which would be better left in total darkness. No light in the world comes upwards from the earth, no architect could have conceived it. But then equally you might say no Bach could have imagined the modern piano; one compromises.'

She thinks that before she dies she would like to live again in a house like these. 'We were so conditioned by Father in his taste – I hate that word, I prefer education. No furniture, for instance, was ever to be set at an angle, it was always straight against the wall. It was like the rule that one should only read good literature before lunch. One had a guilty conscience if one read fiction before the entertainment hours, the drinking hours. Quite idiotic.'

The five Lutyens children had a curious childhood. They watched the gap widen between their mother and father as Mother took up Theosophy

22

and Vegetarianism and Father did not. This is splendidly evoked in Elisabeth Lutyens's autobiography, *A Goldfish Bowl*, where she says: 'In the early days Mother held conventional prayers for the assembled household . . . I remember a young housemaid bursting into tears during the singing of Eternal Father Strong to Save, because that day her young man was crossing to the Isle of Wight.'

'Later, in Theosophical days, incense wafted through the house, while we had to sit in a circle, hands held, and chant "I am a link in a golden chain of love which stretches round the world" before the day's bickering could begin. One day Mother went so far as to exorcise Father in his office, which he bore with his usual patience.'

But Mother was picturesque: coming up to the nursery in a long Fortuné tea-gown of soft accordion-pleated silk; reading aloud to the children every day, knitting all the while. A J. M. Barrie kind of mother; not surprisingly the family treat was a trip to Peter Pan once a year. They must have felt they were watching a home movie.

'Mother was a hopeless hostess,' says Miss Lutyens. 'It's important for an architect to entertain, and Mother had no sense of food. She would say "Would you like some cheese, if there *is* any?" or produce half a bottle of tepid Graves. I mean, in those days, what had women to do, with a nannie to look after the children and a housekeeper to run the house? Mother effectively left Father. You can't have your cake and eat it too.'

In 1919 the family moved to a grander home: to the enormous Adam house in Mansfield Street which bears a blue plaque commemorating the two architects who lived there, John Loughborough Pearson, and Sir Edwin Landseer Lutyens. Part of the Howard de Walden estate, it was sold by Miss Lutyens' late brother Robert only a couple of years ago to become solicitors' offices and luxury flats.

We turn into Mansfield Street past Chandos House in Queen Anne Street. 'Lady Chandos married once for love, once for title, and once for money, which was a howling success,' says Miss Lutyens.

It was in Mansfield Street that Sir Edwin conceived and built Queen Mary's Doll's House, to the great interest of the children.

'I remember Queen Mary visiting Father one afternoon, pulling all the plugs in the miniature lavatories and getting her pearl ear-rings caught in the plumber's moustache as they stooped to check the plumbing.'

When the family came to Mansfield Street the Ormsby-Gores lived on the corner opposite, and Dame Nellie Melba lived next door.

'She drove me mad with her practising. I thought my playing was more important than her singing. I thought her a bloody nuisance. I heard she died from eating water-cress, poor thing.

'I hated this district then because it was so lugubrious at weekends. It was simply a morgue because all the doctors went away.'

Approaching the white front door she notices that the brass lion knocker is still the same one, only very worn and smooth. 'We used to put a piece of toffee on it,' she says, 'and wait for it to melt in the sun.'

It is a vast house. The broad echoing hallway still has Sir Edwin's black and white marble floor, but no longer the dark blue lapis lazuli paint on the walls stretching all the way up the staircase to the superb skylight four floors above.

In the basement, which she later took over as a flat, Elisabeth Lutyens found a huge vaulted Dutch kitchen, with old charcoal ovens, and cheese rooms and wine vaults which could be turned into bedrooms. In the basement alone, she had five living-in staff.

Here in Mansfield Street Elisabeth was prepared for the deb's social life, coming out and presentation at court. Typically, she rebelled against it all, but she learned to love literature at Miss Wolff's day classes in North Audley Street.

In place of her mother, Elisabeth became her father's hostess, especially at the parties he gave at the Garrick Club. He called her Betty-late-than-never. He was fond of puns.

'I am not much of a father in a fatherway,' he wrote to her, 'but you make it up by being a perfect daughter in a daughterly way as I think you aughterly should do.'

Absorbed in his work, he was for seventeen years going back and forth to India, building New Delhi; but she remembers him pretending to play the children like cellos, and making them little crowns out of orange peel for King George V's coronation.

One looks for memories of the Bloomsbury set: she remembers Lady Ottoline Morrell sweeping past in Bedford Square in white chiffon and Lytton Strachey, grandfather's godson, with a squeaky voice, and Maynard Keynes, 'a rather sinister gentleman with a dead white face'.

She knew Vita Sackville-West, and her mother ('mad as a hatter: used to be a great patron of Father's and would pay him in kind. One year she gave him a Mortlake tapestry, another a Rolls-Royce, and then she wanted the things back. Quite cuckoo.') And Yeats came to dinner, 'looking so much the poet, with his long limp hair and floppy tie. He seemed quite devoid of humour. It was sticky going.'

After the visit to her childhood homes, redolent of elegance and privilege, Elisabeth Lutyens reflects on being so ill-prepared by this background for her years struggling for recognition by the musical establishment. During those growing-up years she was never taken to concerts, her family being completely unmusical despite the Bechstein piano in the drawing-room.

'There was no music to be heard at our London homes. Only the barrel organs playing in the streets, and the Salvation Army brass band on a Sunday morning, that unaccountably moved me to tears.

'The amount of concerts that must have been going on in London then, fascinating concerts that I didn't even know about . . .' she says. 'My only conclusion is that you should give children opportunities to do everything.'

CHAPTER FOUR

Ivor Newton
Limehouse

For such an eminent Victorian, who often enthuses on London's past, Ivor Newton was most reluctant to visit the scenes of his childhood. Nothing would induce him, he said, to go back.

'It won't be "How Boy from East End Slums Became Famous Accompanist", will it?' he said. 'You must keep it light-hearted because I'm never very profound or serious myself.'

Eventually he agreed to make his way eastward with me. He affects to forget exactly where his home was ('it's all changed so anyway, after all it was nearly a hundred years ago'), but says he would like to re-visit the church where he was christened. He is intensely proud of the church; on the wall of his music-room in Kinnerton Street hangs a John Piper gouache of the church.

It is St Anne's, Limehouse, one of Nicholas Hawksmoor's noble achievements, whose tower could be seen by all the returning sailors coming up the Thames. It is still an impressive sight, making its surroundings, on the junction of Commercial Road and the East India Dock Road, look the more depressing.

But it is locked and looks neglected. 'Danny O'Lay is a Mug of all Mugs', someone has scrawled on one wall of its sweeping steps. 'In my day,' says Ivor Newton, standing in the churchyard, 'it was gleaming white and beautiful. There were quite a lot of rich people living around here; one saw servants in caps and aprons. Look, even the clock doesn't work. It's three o'clock and what does it say? Eleven.'

'The Salvation Army,' says Ivor Newton, 'was born around here. And Dr Barnardo's. They would pick up children sleeping in doorways without shoes or stockings.'

When Ivor Newton first went to St Anne's he was a baby in the flowing christening robe of lace and ribbons worn by his four elder brothers before him, and by the sixth brother after him. (Three of these six sons were lost in the First World War.)

'I believe that it was Hawksmoor's building, and the music I heard in it, which taught me that there was another and richer world ahead of me,' he says.

As we went down the Whitechapel Road, he remembered how cosmopolitan that area used to be. 'Everyone chattering away in their native languages, from Norwegians to lascars, people who'd arrived at the docks and never moved any further. It was almost exclusively Jewish, of course, and they all talked Yiddish. Now they've all gone to Hampstead.'

We passed the London Opera Centre on Commercial Road – 'used to be a marvellous cinema called the Troxy, in the days of Mary Pickford' – where a rehearsal for Charpentier's *Louise* was in progress. Inside the walls are festooned with historic concert posters, many of them bearing the legend: 'At the piano: Ivor Newton.'

Ivor Newton recalls that during Noel Coward's last year, he went to stay at the Coward house at Les Avents. And Coward introduced him to fellow house guests thus: 'This is Ivor Newton, who has soothed the savage breasts of all the famous singers over the centuries.'

From Commercial Road we made our way towards the river and the Isle of Dogs, along Limehouse Causeway. 'Used to be the area of the opium dens, I believe,' says Ivor. 'You must know the story of the beautiful Florence Leonora Stewart, a sort of Marilyn Monroe of her day, who changed her name to Billie Carleton, because that was thought to be frightfully daring. She was found in her West End flat, dead of an overdose of drugs she got in a Limehouse opium den – run by a Chinese called Ten Ping You.

'Everybody was terribly shocked. It was said she would leave the theatre and make her way along to Limehouse to mix in a circle of degenerates.'

Ivor Newton's Limehouse was, he says, like something drawn by Rowlandson. 'The neighbourhood was so full of activity that it was endlessly fascinating.

'Now look around us. Dead, isn't it? When you consider how near it is to the City. This part of London seems to have everything but inhabitants. Not many people about. The Magnet and Dewdrop, there's an interesting name for a pub. All very *blonde* around here, the girls, aren't they?'

In his childhood, incredibly, Limehouse was a staunch Conservative stronghold. 'Of course the Labour Party didn't exist, and the Liberals were just damned Radicals,' he says. His father was a businessman who would

St Anne's, Limehouse: 'gleaming white and beautiful'

take the boy Ivor along to the local Conservative Club to play the piano at their smoking concerts.

Considering his early promise (by the time he was twelve his bandmaster told him he couldn't teach him any more) he had only moderate encouragement from his parents: as he practised, his mother – who loved to be told she looked like Ellen Terry – would sit reading in the drawing-room, and Ivor would long for praise, but when he asked her what she thought of his playing, she would say, 'It sounded rather dull to me.'

But by the age of ten, the man who later accompanied Tetrazzini, Melba, Clara Butt, and Chaliapin had already played regularly at every town hall east of Aldgate Pump. He played at Sunday League concerts, reciting burlesques of Adelphi melodrama to his own piano accompaniment, sitting half facing the audience in his little Eton suit.

He went to the Guildhall School of Music in the City, and began his long career modestly enough in pierrot shows for summer seasons. But his first job as resident pianist was at the Queen's Palace of Varieties which, as he puts it, 'lurked in a back street in Poplar by the Blackwall Tunnel approach.

'It was the height of music-hall popularity, every suburb had one,' he says, 'and the Queen's was typical Edwardian music-hall. A service-bar at one side and a sort of gin-palace at the other, very ornate, where the proprietor and his sons would hold court.'

Young Ivor was shocked to see how many women brought babies with them, and fed them with sips of beer. Here he played for Marie Lloyd and Vesta Tilley – 'the music-hall was entirely democratic: they played in the West End and then came along to Poplar as well'.

Still, he kept his music-hall nights a secret, playing serious music during the day and then sneaking off to the Queen's at night, a long and alarming walk home through dark and empty streets. 'No one I knew ever heard me at the Queen's, and I never told Arthur Barclay [his professor at the Guildhall] that I was so menially occupied.'

He has always been a walker and an observer. 'I remember May Day processions, where I saw probably the last Green Man, survivor of Merrie Olde England, all covered in spring leaves. And the marvellous colourful cavalcades out to Epsom and Ascot, everyone turning out in their smartest clothes.'

He can't get over the quietness of the area now, apart from the ceaseless traffic noise. 'The noises of my childhood were human,' he says. 'Not jet engines and juggernauts and gears grinding, but horses and carts, muffin men's bells, newsboys with placards shouting. There was a barrel organ on every corner, and German bands playing all the time, so when there was any rejoicing, like Mafeking night, everybody came out on the streets and sang and danced.'

It had its gruesome side as well of course. 'I remember a Limehouse street fight when an Irishman was knocked down on the pavement and killed, in a quantity of blood. And every night his unfortunate widow would make her way to the blood-stained spot, kneel down and loudly wail her prayers for his soul.'

And he remembers the utter silence, too, that suddenly descended the night Queen Victoria died. 'I was about nine, and it was incredibly fascinating and frightening,' he says. 'People spoke only in awe-struck whispers. I was forbidden to touch the piano that night for the first time in my life. My mother, like everyone else, went into mourning and we all understood that an historic age had come to an end.'

Once, the boy Ivor tried to run to sea, fancying himself playing the piano on a Cunard liner, and answered an ad in *The Stage*. But his Victorian head-of-family father said, 'Nonsense!' and that was that. On another occasion he made a secret visit to the Theatre Royal, Stratford, then famous for blood-and-thunder melodrama, to take part in a music competition.

29

'I wore a knickerbocker suit, and played a piece with flashy variations, and won first prize,' says Ivor. 'The prize was a large gold signet ring, so large it slipped off and I lost it at once.

'The greatest thrill for me was travelling in the front seat of a horse bus. Every bus driver seemed to be a Toby Weller, whose *obiter dicta* was treasured by passengers near him. Once I remember a driver forming his whip into the shape of a noose as another driver went by, and then explaining, " 'Is brother was 'anged this morning." Victorians were much tougher and less compassionate than people today.

'For one thing, they were much too vital and lively to ever think of forming a queue. One literally had to fight one's way into the cheapest seats at a theatre. It was much more exciting than queueing.'

As a boy he thought the zenith of architectural achievement was the Mansion House. 'I longed to go inside. It was my greatest ambition. Now of course I've played there many times.

'Victorian characters were bigger and richer,' he says. 'Everyone dressed their part in life. You could tell a coster the moment you saw him. An actor looked like an actor, with his black hat and floppy tie. Look, there's an actor, you could say. Well brought up little boys like me wore sailor suits. Musicians had luxuriant masses of hair.

'And of course everyone, but everyone, wore a hat. Even little street urchins without shoes wore a grubby cap. To say, "I'm sure his mother never wore a hat," was like saying, "I'm sure his mother drinks gin." '

Ivor Newton still wears a hat, and a jolly little figure he looks in it, too.

'The most extraordinary sight of my childhood in Limehouse,' he says, 'was the Chinamen who wore pigtails and coolie hats and blue smocks down to their knees, flapping silk trousers and strange shoes, and a stick with two baskets across their shoulders. Can you imagine it? Nowadays simply everybody looks like a bank clerk.'

CHAPTER FIVE

Monica Dickens
Notting Hill

Monica Dickens is uncompromising about the area of London where she was born. 'Notting Hill Gate,' she says, 'is the hub of the universe.'

The great-granddaughter of Charles Dickens was born in 1915 in a handsome double-fronted house built about 1800, that stands squarely on the corner of the Portobello Road, just where the market begins, in Chepstow Villas.

Absurdly enough, living in Chepstow Villas was in her day a deeply shaming thing. 'Oh, it was a very bad neighbourhood. When my parents bought the house in 1912 it was quite respectable. Then it came to be like Clapham – only Clapham is OK now, isn't it – right on the edge of the London slums. In the unlikely event of any guy asking to take me home, I would be too ashamed to say I lived in Chepstow Villas. Of course now it's madly chic again.'

The Dickens parents lived there until only a few years ago, so Monica has seen it go through its many degrees of modishness.

'In my day most of the houses had degenerated into rooming houses, full of alcoholic boxers. There was a brothel across the street. Ours was the only family house on the block, very shabby-genteel. The streets began to be a centre for all kinds of strange occult sects, with weird signs on the doors; failures and revolutionaries and penniless students and odd, potty people lived there.'

In the fifties she saw it go through its teddy-boy period, and the race riots when the concentration of immigrants north of Portobello turned it into a combat area. 'And in my youth,' she says, 'it was considered to be out in the sticks. It seemed a tremendous trek to get anywhere. Now it's the navel of the world.'

To get there from her present London home, off Queen's Gate (most of

Portobello Road '. . . always sort of wandered northwards, getting worse and worse'

the year she lives in a white Colonial house at Cape Cod), we cross Notting
Hill Gate: the Gaumont, formerly the Coronet, memorable for cowboy
films; Bland's the umbrella shop, quite changeless; and the Caprini café,
formerly a peculiar old shop where Monica as a girl of twelve coveted a
pair of brown riding boots in the window.

'It used to say: "Secondhand Clothes, Misfits, Uniforms, Waiters,
Weddings, Riding Clothes Bought And Sold." I once went in there and
found the boots were much too large, being men's. But what do you think,
the shop still exists, only moved round the corner.'

Anyone who has read Miss Dickens' novel, *The Heart of London* (reissued
in 1973 by Heinemann) will recognize the neighbourhood and the house.
Even the boots feature in the story: 'When Martha (the heroine) was
twelve and hungry for horses, the boots had called to her every time she
passed them.'

The end of Portobello Road evokes walks home from St Paul's school,
in many different moods; and going to church, at Brompton Oratory or at
St Mary of the Angels, known as Smelly Angels, which is how it sounds if
you say it quickly.

The house, full of ghosts of Christmases past, scene of huge family parties each Christmas because the Dickens family was enormous, stands dressed now in a pale blue wash, instead of its former cream: 'A terrifically comfortable house, but terribly unsmart. It used to belong to someone called Bonaparte, a relative of Napoleon, which seemed to us immensely impressive.'

Much of the house is under siege by builders, since the present owners, Mr and Mrs Charles Baring ('oodles of money; they own a bank') are extending it upwards with another storey. It is clearly still a happy family house with William Morris-design wallpapers everywhere.

'Ah, this hallway. I can remember so many times creeping in at night without any shoes, avoiding the creaking boards *here*, and *here*, to avoid waking the parents.' Where had she been, out so late? 'Oh, to Quag's, to hear the big bands.'

The drawing-room still has its fireplace and its plasterwork frieze of scrolls and urns and leaves, once thoroughly black but now gleaming white. 'My mother would sit exactly here, on the sofa,' says Miss Dickens, 'with her little cocktail and her mending-basket.

'Charles Dickens's desk used to sit in that corner, the one from his house at Gad's Hill, now in Doughty Street. I used to sit at the desk and hope for inspiration. I wrote *One Pair Of Hands* [her first best-seller] in here, in three weeks, writing by hand in a notebook like Jane Austen.'

And the room which was her father's workroom has become an Ideal Home-style kitchen. From the window you can see the remains of the air-raid shelter in the garden. 'My mother and father would dine in the shelter every night, and one night my father was just carrying a decanter of port and a bowl of walnuts out there, it being September, when an oil-bomb fell in the next door garden. He just made it through the doorway of the shelter with the decanter in one hand, saying, "Thank God the port's all right."

'There used to be a white line on the garden wall, for practising tennis. And my father invented a game that was a mixture of cricket and squash. Every Sunday about twenty of his friends would come over for a game of stump cricket.'

The house has two other views. From the day nursery upstairs you can see the pink house over the road that Miss Dickens swears used to be a brothel. And from her mother's bedroom, the room where Monica was born (straw being spread over the road outside, to muffle the horses' hooves), the window over Portobello Road where the two sisters would signal to their friends, forbidden street ruffians.

One of these boys was known to Monica always as Arry Asker. Only years later did she learn that his name was Harry Housego.

Fashionable improvements have replaced the delft china bowls and wooden seats in the house's four lavatories, and replaced the basement's pantries and wine cellars and scullery complete with back-breaking stone sink, with a children's den and *au pair*'s rooms. 'Gosh, I wish the house had been as warm as this when I was here. No radiators, of course, just a gas fire over which one crouched, holding out one's pants to warm them.' Also gone: the tubes in all the rooms down which one could whistle and blow the cook's ear off.

Naturally all the servants had memorable names. A sewing lady, who had been their grandmother's lady's maid, called Annie Bavin. Cook was Minnie Maunder from Devonshire; Nannie, around whom life revolved, was Ethel May Gathergood from Norfolk.

'Every family picture in those days centred on the nannie, and one's cousins' nannies. It was extremely cosy because nannies had nothing whatever to do but answer our foolish questions.

'My parents were told that they could not marry until they could afford two servants,' says Miss Dickens. 'So they were engaged for four years and it never occurred to them to get married before that.

'After the wedding, they were driving away from the church, and my mother turned to my father and said, "*Now* will you tell me what Oscar Wilde did?" He'd promised he would tell her only after they were married.'

Outside the house the market is in full cry. 'It got a bit much, when the market moved up here,' says Miss Dickens. 'One could never find a parking place.' Exactly what happened: our car got blocked into the driveway of the house. So Miss Dickens promptly executed a brilliant nine-point turn and drove it out along the pavement to the accompaniment of bravos from a policeman and two traffic wardens.

'I know this driveway intimately,' she said. 'In my youth I drove my dashing SS sports car, with its huge long nose, right through this gate and got it so tightly jammed that when I sobered up I couldn't back it out again. It stayed there for about three months.'

Outside the house a little Italian used to sell his paintings on Saturday mornings, lined against the garden railings. 'My father would stand on the steps and rage at him. "Oh Meester Deekens, you my friend," he would say. "You and I have gin together." And they always ended up having gin together, after all the vociferous argument.'

The shop directly opposite, on Portobello Road, is Roger's Antiques, which used to be their newsagent's. Next door to the house is that odd little place, the Centaur Gallery, full of icons and bric-à-brac now, which used to house a little man who repaired shoes. 'He might well have been over six feet tall,' says Miss Dickens, 'but inevitably he was known as a little man.'

Opposite again is Trad, the fairground relics shop of Lord and Lady Bangor, which used to be a sweet shop. 'I have an old roundabout-top,' says Miss Dickens, 'in my tack room. It says "Long Safe Ride" on one side, and "Longest Ride in the Fair" on the other.'

We wander among the shops and stalls crammed with bygones and memorabilia, stopping to buy a china nightlight for her sister, and a pound of sprouts at the vegetable-stall end. 'Portobello, known as the Lane, has always sort of wandered northwards, getting worse and worse,' she says. 'The shops were always small-time, and the houses were the homes of servants and grooms of all the big houses in Bayswater. It was rather like the East End in that it was always a cheerful, fun street, never depressing.'

In her day the stalls were rag-and-bone and vegetables, not antiques, and the market didn't begin until the other side of Westbourne Grove. 'My mother used to shop there, which was considered very progressive. Anyone who was anyone got their groceries from Whiteleys or Barkers, who would call at the back door for the order.'

Only the pub names remain from those days, the Princess Alexandra and the Earl of Lonsdale 'where the bus drivers from the No 15 used to dash down the alley and spend a penny'. Stallholders' spelling is as imaginative as ever: 'Advacado's', 'Confrence lovely eatin' pear's, sweet and juicey'. She remembers the Electric Cinema Club, mecca of film buffs, as being first a pre-talkie cinema with piano, and later a Salvation Army hall.

'There were stables all along the back of the street full of costermongers' ponies, the first ponies I ever got to know.' The devotion to horses lingers; immediately after our Portobello visit she was off to open a home of rest for old pit-ponies in Basildon.

'As late as 1942 I remember buying a harness down the Portobello Road, for a pony that I thought had been broken into harness. We hitched it to a governess cart at Windsor and it was furious, and kicked the cart in and spilled all my sister's children into the road, fracturing their nannie's skull.'

Back to the house, and memories of the vast family gatherings at Christmas, with about twenty cousins on each side, and grandparents, all converging on their house because her parents were such welcoming and gregarious people. Grandfather was Charles Dickens's son Henry, who lived like all the Dickenses to the great age of eighty-four and then stepped off a pavement in Cheyne Walk, holding out his hand as old men do, and was run down by a motorbike.

'It's almost haunted by love, this house,' reflects Monica Dickens. 'That's something everybody always feels about it.'

35

Some day, she says, there will be a blue plaque on her house, as there is on a house across the road. 'You have to be dead first,' I remind her pleasantly. 'Do you? The swine,' she says. We cross to see who lived over the road. 'Louis Kossuth, 1802–94, Hungarian patriot, stayed here.' 'Who he?' cries Miss Dickens. 'I'm sure if he's got one, I can have one, too.' Quite right.

CHAPTER SIX

Philip Hope-Wallace
Wimbledon

'And is there tennis still for tea?' wondered Philip Hope-Wallace, the writer and *Guardian* critic, thinking back to his childhood in Wimbledon. He once said, in a nostalgic article: 'I dare say very much more of that world survives than I imagine . . . but I haven't the heart to go and see.'

Take heart, I said, and we went to see. He was right: Wimbledon is as Wimbledon was. There wasn't tennis, it being November, but there were hot buttered roasted chestnuts for tea in the house that was the Hope-Wallace home for forty-nine years.

Not only was the large, solid, respectable late-Victorian house still there, in its quiet cul-de-sac off Lancaster Road; but it is still a family house.

It has only ever been occupied by four families since 1888 – the Alexanders, the Hope-Wallaces, the Powell-Evanses and currently the Cuppages (parents, five children and a housekeeper) who so hospitably offered us tea. So much for Harrod's estate agents, who told Hope-Wallace in 1952 that there was no call for such houses nowadays.

Philip Hope-Wallace, 'Writer, Critic, Wit' as the plaque on the wall of a Fleet Street wine-bar puts it (causing people to remark that he has become a legend in his own lunch-time) is a raconteur. And every turning, every view on the route through Wimbledon, sparked off the racontage.

We passed the house where Watts-Dunton rescued the poet Swinburne from alcoholism, and I was told how Swinburne once kissed Philip Hope-Wallace's sister Nina (now Lady Hoare) in her pram, causing their Alsatian nannie to raise her umbrella aloft and rain blows upon the poet's head. That was Mrs Lutz, sent away at the outbreak of the First World War because Hope-Wallace *père* did not wish to be harbouring a Hun. Philip remembers her weeping and packing her trunks.

We journey past the misty expanse of the Common, still ringed by the

Lancaster Road: 'always Sunday afternoon'

grand houses that Osbert Lancaster terms Wimbledon Transitional; *fin de siècle* monolithic piles with occasional eighteenth-century mansions, a perfect rentiers' paradise as Philip Hope-Wallace calls it.

'It summons recollections of going out to tea in the four-wheeled growler hired from Dormer's, smelling of hay and dung and driven by a drunken coachman, with one's satin slippers in a bag embroidered "Slippers", and being too shy to get out, urged by one's mother "Oh do come on, you know all the people, it'll be a lovely party, beautiful food." '

Wimbledon in that time was much less a suburb than a village. 'It seemed much farther from London then. It used to take a good hour: one drove to Putney Bridge with an open top, then took the District Line. And it was villagey. It had its own life and culture. I suppose we considered ourselves rather poor, always keeping up appearances.'

All the roads around the Common bring forth their ghosts. In Court-hope Gardens lived the Miss Stracheys, 'whose father had been court chamberlain at Dresden, and with whom I used to go for German walks in order to learn the language . . . and just near here we had a marvellous murder, the first *crime passionnel* of the First World War, when Captain Malcolm returned from Flanders to find his wife in bed with an Anglo-Catholic pacifist decorator.'

The Common is more overgrown than formerly, but still conserved by the Conservators and ranged by the Forest Rangers, who wear brown bowlers and gaiters.

On the Common, Philip and his sister were left under the trees by the

Alsatian nannie, while she and another nannie ran to see the suffragettes being ducked in the Rushmere. Here, too, you could see balloons, and the first flying-machines, a sight at which Philip's mother shrieked to a friend: 'Run, Edie, run – it's the sight of your life!' and Edie ran, in her hobble skirt.

Here is the Pound, where they corralled the stray horses and ponies, and the War Memorial which was a sort of Speakers' Corner, and the Windmill 'where Henry VIII stopped while hunting, and listened to hear the cannon which indicated that Anne Boleyn's head had rolled'.

'Up near the Mill, at a certain point, you could hear the thump of the barrage in Flanders,' says Hope-Wallace. 'And it used to make our English nannie cry because she had a brother at the front.'

On Bank Holidays the whole of South London, it seemed, would congregate there. The rest of the year the Common was everything that was not 'common' – 'walking, picnicking, wonderful skating in the winter, and lots of horse-riding'.

'Here, as a little boy, I was made to distribute cigarettes to the soldiers. Two to the sergeants and one to the others. I hated that, the feeling of dispensing charity.'

Miss Frost's the newsagent's is still there, though Miss Frost must by now have, as PH-W puts it, 'joined the majority'. It is still called Frost's. And the Dog and Fox, then as now the popular village pub, was known to be the place you could always get a meal in an emergency. Not that the Hope-Wallaces would go into pubs, 'except at Christmas time, to get a teaspoonful of brandy for the pudding'.

We pass by King's College School, where Philip went until they discovered he couldn't read, he claims, and dispatched him to prep school at Eastbourne (where he was a contemporary of A. J. Ayer), thence to Charterhouse, to Europe and to Balliol. Opposite the school still is the Crooked Billet, on the very edge of the Common, and everywhere beyond there were fields, and woods with nightingales.

And there, in Lancaster Way, a leafy cul-de-sac behind Wimbledon Village, is the house: smaller than he remembered it, less laurel-encrusted than formerly, with a new-fangled car-port at the side. But there are the little pillars off which the young Philip often fell, and the same front door which he barricaded against the bombs, using a huge mahogany bookcase full of bound *Punches* as well as sandbags.

'Solidly constructed, you see,' he says. 'Our family came there in 1910, and my parents built on that side-kitchen because they didn't think it natural to imprison Irish girls down there in the area, the basement' (there were always two Irish maids, a nannie, a bootboy and a nurserymaid). 'I

was born in another house: I don't know why, they were probably building this kitchen at the time.'

Life was comfortable; at the back, rich people like Durlacher, the Bond
Street art dealer; across the road the Strain family, whose daughter Jean
married the present Archbishop of York.

'A great colony of theosophists lived nearby, who caused much scandal,
and there were endless musical parties where people drank fearfully strong
things like tea. Dancing was the thing, and church-going too, the two
inextricably mixed because dancing classes were held in all the church halls.
And then, of course, came tennis.'

The Hope-Wallaces built their own tennis court in the back garden,
cutting down a cedar tree to do so. 'It used to be known as *the* tennis,
something you watched from nannie's shoulder over the privet hedge at
Worple Road, Mrs Lambert Chambers serving underhand to an opponent
in a hairnet, a petersham belt and a long flannel skirt.

'And then suddenly along came a lady named Suzanne Lenglen, with her
legs and her bandeau, and Queen Mary was so taken with her that she came
back and back, and they moved the whole thing and built the new stadium.

'Then all the houses had lunch parties with salmon and raspberries and
cream. My father, I remember, was offered debenture shares in Wimbledon
that entitled him to ten Centre Court seats in perpetuity. But he turned
them down. It was just a silly fad, he said, it'd all be over in no time.'

The tennis court is gone from the back garden but otherwise every stone
is familiar. No more herbaceous borders, but it's still the same garden
roller (of course – nobody ever removes a garden roller) and the same
verandah and the same fig-tree and the same Anderson shelter.

But the poplars are felled, farewell to the shade, as Cowper said; and the
uninterrupted view from the garden towards the Jacobean Eagle House
(built by Sir Thomas Jackson, who rebuilt The High in Oxford) is now
obscured. The Comice pear trees have gone, and the old garden fence (off
which the unsteady young Philip also fell) itself fell down last year, to be
replaced by a neat wall.

Inside the house, Philip Hope-Wallace points out to the present children
the very good banisters for sliding on, the very solid doors for pulling out
milk teeth on a piece of string. The mantelpiece in the drawing-room came
from his grandfather's house at Box Hill 'in the garden cottage of which
George Meredith lived and died'.

'My father's family,' he explains, 'were landed gentry who'd come down
in the world. He was born in a castle in Northumberland, so this house
was crowded with stuff, an enormous mirror here, a spinning-wheel there,
and here in the dining-room there was a huge hideous marble fireplace.

Enormous family feasts, like something out of Priestley, were staged in here.

'I remember the Christmas of 1943 in here, when we had frightful cold, and no food, and no drink, but we made do.'

There is a window on the first landing from which the children could be lifted up to peer through a telescope and amazingly, read the time on the face of Big Ben. And a table in one of the bedrooms where Philip had his tonsils out, all such surgery being carried out at home then. Hide and seek was played in the linen-cupboard.

'Goodness,' said Philip Hope-Wallace. 'I shall see ghosts tonight.'

We took tea in the study, where the window seat once formed such a natural box for seating the Hope-Wallace parents, while they were treated to theatrical performances of Grimm's Fairy Tales by the three children, groaning at the long stage-waits.

'And my parents used to hold a Shakespeare Reading Society here, for about twenty years,' he said, 'entirely in order that my mother could read all the best female parts and father all the best male parts.

'When they did *Antony and Cleopatra* I remember my mother read Cleopatra and my father not only read Antony but Enobarbus as well. When a lady complained that all she ever got was messengers' parts, and all she'd had to say was "What, ho, without?" they held a sort of post-mortem, and my father said, in a great indication of the unabashed snobbery of the time, "Well, what does she expect? She's only a builder's daughter!"'

For Philip Hope-Wallace, Wimbledon represents halcyon summers: and truly it still suggests a timeless ease, that area around the Common.

'What an experiment in gracious upper-class living it was,' he says. 'What a memory of hot Sunday afternoons it leaves – always Sunday afternoon, with the elders sleeping off the beef in deck-chairs under cedars.'

CHAPTER SEVEN

Sam Oddy
Paddington

Sam Oddy is sadly missed in Paddington Green. Until 1973 he was there twice a week with his fruit and vegetable van, as he had been for more than fifty years; man, boy and baby. When Sam was born, in 1919, his mother would take him in her basket with her on the fruit cart; just as his father had been taken on his father's cart and his grandfather before that.

Sam's family have been costermongers since the early nineteenth century. 'So I do know a cabbage from a lettuce,' says Sam (large wink). He was born right down by the Grand Union Canal, at Paddington Basin. The family had a sort of farmhouse on North Wharf Road, on the site where the Sarah Siddons Girls' School now stands.

'My granny had a cottage there, where she had seventeen children; sixteen boys and one girl,' says Sam. 'Well there was no television in those days.'

Sam's father, Tom Oddy, bought a donkey and a brightly painted cart in the early 1900s. He and his bride of eighteen used to go to Covent Garden at three every morning, walking alongside the donkey, pick the best fruit and take up their stand on Paddington Green.

Later the donkey-cart became a pony van with a hooped roof and the donkey was replaced by Ginger, a young pony who got to be famous around Paddington. He lived to the age of thirty-one.

'Ol' Ginger came out of the Welsh mines, blind he was,' says Sam. 'They used to prick their eyeballs to make them go down the mines.' A row of brass and silver medals from the London Van Horse Parades in the late twenties and early thirties, held in Regent's Park or at Hounslow or Olympia hang down by Sam's fireplace, testifying to Ginger's merit.

We walked from Sam's present home, a sunny council flat under the spire of St Augustine's Church, Maida Vale, to revisit the spot where Sam and his fruit-van stood every Wednesday and Saturday all these years in the entrance of the churchyard of St Mary's, Paddington Green. This is the church where he and all his family were both christened and married; his grandson Spencer was the first baby to be christened there since the expensive and controversial restoration of the church in 1973.

St Mary's dates from 1791, but in the church that preceded it Hogarth married Jane Thornhill, and in the church that preceded that, John Donne preached. Sam is proud of these historic associations.

Standing in the churchyard in the centre of Paddington Green the dominant feature everywhere is the Westway which streaks by, obliterating most things and slicing the area so divisively that to get over to Sam's old home by the canal we have to take a long loop round by Edgware Road Tube Station, the ABC and the new Hotel Metropole.

'The Green gardens,' says Sam, 'used to extend right out across there, before the motorway came. Paddington Borough, as it then was, used to have wonderful flower beds with different pictures in flowers every season. And in that one block, right opposite, there used to be *eight* pubs.'

Still, there are relics of the Green that Polly Perkins knew (pretty Polly Perkins of Paddington Green, of course: Sam's granny remembered her. Her house still stands near the children's hospital). There is the 1873 church hall of St Mary's, known in Sam Oddy's childhood as the Rag School, which became, in 1959, the 59 club for ton-up boys. And there is the statue of Sarah Siddons, derived from Reynolds' portrait, though her cottage here, Westbourne Farm, was demolished in 1860.

And across on North Wharf Road there are still cottages that remain from Sam's day. 'Our yard,' he says, 'used to take up half the area the Sarah Siddons School covers. During the summer we all used to sleep outside in the yard. There were shelters and loose-boxes for hansom cabs and horses, about nine or ten of them, and I used to have to ride the horses bareback to the blacksmith's to be shod at six bob a set. There's only one blacksmith left in Paddington now: Wally Baker, in Junction Mews.'

Sitting on the wall of the canal, Sam remembers: 'Every Easter they used to run all this water away and scrub the bottom of the Basin. And all the goods that used to come into these warehouses here, timber, sand, bricks, ballast, would be towed by horses along the towpaths.'

A couple of the old narrow-boats are moored at the canal-side. One belongs to the nearby Beauchamp Lodge Settlement, a local charitable community centre (old people's clubs, nursery, disco) which every year organizes holidays for deprived children on the old barges along the inland waterways.

Sam Oddy's fruit and vegetable cart at St Mary's, Paddington Green

'The barge families used to live on these boats,' says Sam.

'And back in the thirties there was a spit-and-sawdust beer-house here in this yard, the Royal Oak, known as the Blue because it always had a blue light. It was a right old jolly-up every Saturday night. They would all go in there, the bargees, after doing their shopping in Church Street Market.

'You could live for a week on a pound then, when a pound was a pound.'

It is just a few hundred yards from the much more grand stuccoed houses of peaceful Little Venice, the oasis of trees and waterway that reminds you of how rural Paddington was before the coming of the railway and then the motorway. Sam takes me into the Warwick, a nice old Victorian pub half obscured by the road network, to see the murals of old Paddington.

They are strange drawings: Youths in baker-boy caps fishing in the canal, captioned: 'You won't catch no fish here.' 'No fish? I like that. Why, Captain Cheshire the Cheesemonger of our Corps caught one about a week ago almost as long as my hand.'

'It really was a quiet area, once,' says Sam. 'It was a novelty to see a man ride up Harrow Road on a bicycle. On Sunday afternoons at tea-time you would hear the old muffin man ringing his bell and after him the shellfish man shouting out, and round about five o'clock the old lamplighter lighting the gas lamps. Just opposite us was the Marylebone Council and the lamplighter would have to knock up all the dustmen in the morning, tapping on their windows with his pole.'

Sam Oddy has served many of the famous in his time. In his biography of Sir John Barbirolli, Michael Kennedy tells how Sir John on coming out of Bart's Hospital, 'had daily visits from his friend the Cockney greengrocer Sam Oddy, "my mate" as Sir John called him, with whom he liked to talk in richest Cockney. Sam's company was a source of real pleasure.'

Sam says: 'Whenever I was round there, he'd pull me in for a drink. He didn't care who was there, a Lady-in-Waiting to the Queen, a Harley Street doctor, he was one of those blokes.' And similarly, Lady Barbirolli talks in warmest terms about Sam: she, like all his customers, says what a rare person he is, kindness itself.

When the war was over and Sam came home from the army, he held a party for all the children orphaned by the war in Paddington. The old ladies of St John's Wood, blind, infirm, would depend on him bringing the best selection of fruit up to them. He would provide flowers for all the old people's homes opposite his.

And back in 1957 the *Guardian* was writing about his mother, then in her seventies and still out every day with the van: 'If you buy a punnet of strawberries from her cart, you don't need to shake it up to see if squashed or unripe berries are below; they will be good from top to bottom.'

Now, since Sam had to give up for health reasons, it is the end of the business altogether, for Sam's son John went into the Post Office from school, and became a Postman Higher Grade at Luton. 'I really thought he might take over, but they don't want street trading any more, there's no future in it,' says Sam affably.

'I never thought of doing anything but going on with the trade. I was born into it, know what I mean?

'I remember when the old dears used to come out to the cart, not with a basket, but a bucket for the potatoes. Or they'd pull their aprons up and you'd chuck it all into their aprons. They'd ask for a penny of pot 'erbs – carrots, onions, celery, everything that went into the soup for a penny.'

Sam remembers his street-cries about his wares mixing with the other cries of lavender, or knives to grind, scissors to mend.

In Sam's generation, all the cousins went into the same business, and all their wives automatically joined in, too. Annie Oddy, Sam's German wife whom he met in München-Gladbach during the war, willingly helped out on busy days after Sam's mother died.

Today, Sam is a porter and odd-job man. He thinks it's a wonderful job. But he does miss Covent Garden and life on the cart. He still goes to

Covent Garden for the fruit for his family (he has two adopted daughters now) and the children's families.

'On my last day in Paddington Green,' says Sam, 'there were so many tears, I came home at the end of the day and I said "I'm glad that's over, I feel so choked myself." But it was either chucking in the job or going to see the Man Above.'

CHAPTER EIGHT

Sir Victor Pritchett
Dulwich, Bermondsey

Sir Victor Pritchett, the writer and critic, grew up in many different Londons. His childhood was as unstable, as mobile and as various as London itself. Not for him the solid background of a particular area: the Pritchetts drifted from suburb to suburb, as he recorded in his autobiography, *A Cab at the Door*.

Still, he discovered for himself in his boyhood what London meant to him, and in his seventies he derives intense pleasure from his knowledge of a lesser known city. He is apt to take foreign visitors on a Pritchett's Tour that no guide-book could devise.

Mother was 'a rootless London pagan, a fog-worshipper, brought up on the folklore of the North London streets'; father was a Mr Micawber figure, bankrupt at twenty-two but one of Nature's salesmen, strutting through life restlessly seeking new commercial enterprises, always nattily dressed and optimistic that something would turn up.

Their married life was a constant upheaval from suburb to suburb, their homes a series of small red-brick Victorian villas, cluttered with potted palms and ornaments with mottoes. Before too long in one place, the cabbie and his horse would be coughing together at the door; a drive to the Underground station, a new home in any of the interchangeable suburbs, Palmers Green, Balham, Uxbridge, Acton, Ealing, Hammersmith, Camberwell, Woodford, Dulwich, Bromley.

Each time they moved, mother would cry, and father would sing, 'Oh dry those tears, oh calm those fears, life will be brighter tomorrow,' and would then set himself up like a princeling in his new domain. At Uxbridge he would walk grandly along the canal towpath in Cowes blazer and cream trousers; at Ealing the house had a tiny three-foot balcony, so he decided he would take breakfast on it, fancying himself on the Riviera.

Sir Victor Pritchett's summer-house in Clive Road, Dulwich:
reading Wordsworth on the roof

But wherever they drifted, the young V. S. Pritchett was excited by his
surroundings, and felt instinctively that he belonged to London. 'Camberwell was slummy and noisy, but boys of ten are energetic and curious and
I loved just wandering from street to street. I was enchanted by the lurid
quality of industrial London.'

Next door in Camberwell was a bakery humming with machinery; nearby was the roar and the shrieks of the Camberwell Roller Skating Rink.
London's pre-motorcar noises are still vivid to Sir Victor. 'The horse
traffic was as dense as motor traffic, and the horses often ran into each
other, or they would run away. The bolting horse was always an excitement, and those who gave chase were heroes.

'The noise of wheels on cobbles was extraordinary, and the smell of
sweating horses and manure pervaded everything. I longed to be one of
the scavenger boys who ran about with a brush and pan, sweeping up;
they wore wide-brimmed hats and lived so dangerously.'

One of the more lasting homes of his childhood, to which we returned
together, was in the pleasant green suburb of Dulwich. To No 200

Clive Road we went – another red-brick Victorian villa, but taller than others they had rented. This one cost sixteen shillings a week, at which father complained bitterly, even though his embroidered cushions and tea-cosies were selling well just then to Harrod's and Liberty's.

It is now, we found, the home of a sculptor named John Cotter. On pedestals around the house now there were assorted breasts and buttocks, navels and faces of lithe ladies, for Mr Cotter had developed a method of casting moulds in silicone rubber of faces and bodies. Sir Victor said his father would have been fascinated to see all these.

Upstairs in the attic, where Sir Victor and brother Cyril would sit at the window and shoot with water-pistols at passers-by, there is now a work-shop crowded with Mr Cotter's inventive creations, such as two identical face-moulds kissing each other, entitled Self-Kiss.

Out in the garden, Sir Victor was delighted to discover that his old summer-house was still there – a little gem of a Secret Garden conical hut made of knobbly tree bark, with superb stained-glass windows. 'I have a great feeling fo that summer-house,' he said. 'At the age of ten I used to sit on top of it, reading Wordsworth.'

Outside the french windows on the paved patio, was another well-remembered object: the old lavatory bowl from the house. It has now be-come an arty plant-pot. Great amusement from Sir Victor. 'I must say the whole garden is in much better condition. My father hated trees. He killed the lilac, destroyed the laburnum tree, it was a wrecked garden. This stretch was absolutely rough and kicked to bits.

'The suburbs then,' said Sir Victor, 'were places where even modest people had interesting literary pretensions. When we were here, on one side of us we had Mr Carter, an ardent Fabian Socialist. He had a modest job on the borough council, but was terribly *avant-garde*, an educated man with a splendid collection of all the Greek classics.

'Next door on the other side was a rather Bohemian family, the O'Dwyers. The wife was French, a fat blowsy lady, an unusual house-keeper – I remember seeing the ashes of the fire raked out on to the carpet – but very learned in French literature, always discussing Racine and Montesquieu with me.

'She would box with her two sons in the garden, roaring with laughter; and when they took exams she made them work very hard, and wrapped cold towels round their heads to keep their brains cool.'

His local school was Rosendale Road elementary. The building is typical 1899 London School Board in appearance.

Sir Victor was happy here, under the enlightened schooling of a Mr Bartlett, who had revolutionary teaching ideas for 1911. He used the Dalton system, free from textbooks and rigid learning by rote, and opened Pritchett's young mind to contemporary poets, and to the invaluable notion of keeping a writer's notebook. The seed was sown: it was at Rosendale Road that V. S. Pritchett decided to become a writer.

The present headmaster, delighted to welcome the famous Old Boy, produced for us some old school photographs. They revealed that where Sir Victor had always thought the then headmaster, Mr Timms, to be at least ninety, with his frock-coat and whiskers, he must have been around forty. 'He would arrive every morning surrounded by a cortège of children fighting to hold his hand; he seemed like God and his attendants.'

He spent all his free time at the Horniman Museum and the Dulwich art gallery, and won a school prize of a book by Ruskin for a drawing of the amulets in the Horniman. From here, he went on to Alleyn's School, fees then £11 a year.

First term began as usual, with embarrassment. Father did not take him along until weeks after term began, declaring that his time was more valuable than any schoolmaster's; and he had to wear his father's Savile Row suits unskilfully cut down, father insisting that nobody would dictate a uniform to him.

But the budding scholar, critic and novelist, though prepared to work with Puritan fervour at his studies, was not destined to have the education he longed for. It was decided at home quite arbitrarily, on the day his grandfather was derailed on the Manchester–London express, that he must leave school at fifteen and go into the leather trade.

In fact, with his customary talent for investing even the most stultifying aspects of his boyhood with interest and amusement, he gained enormous delight from his four years in the leather business in Bermondsey. He had begun to be depressed by suburban life: 'When I looked at the streets and houses around us, the unending stretches of London villas, the great buildings, the Town Halls, my spirits fell.

'I had been born into a family that was isolated – it seemed to me – from all the amenities that I had read of in English literature.' Bermondsey, at least, had novelty, strangeness, an aura of esoteric knowledge. We re-took that journey he had made at fifteen, in stiff collar and bowler, to Weston Street, SE1, then as now the traditional centre of the London leather trade.

'There was a daylight gloom in this district of London,' wrote Sir Victor. 'There was always fog hanging like sour breath in these tunnels.'

The smells, he remembered, were of hops, boots and dog dung. In the fellmongers yard in Bermondsey Street that we visited, the smell was enough to make me reel – an overpowering alkali, like very bad eggs. It reeked from the troughs of depilating liquid, as the sheepskins – great towering heaps of them – were stripped of their wool.

'It was a lovely trade to work in,' said Sir Victor as we were shown round by Mr Rawle of Strong, Rawle and Strong. 'I was absolutely absorbed in it. It was so close to nature.'

His work was not, however, in such a yard as this, of freshly slaughtered skins and troughs of nameless substances. He was in the office, among the high stools and ledgers, the mahogany desks and green lampshades.

But, however fascinating the work, he was infinitely more invigorated by the London outside. At this period he began to explore London. He gave up the Dining Rooms for lunch, and instead went on prolonged safaris down the Old Kent Road, to Fleet Street to gaze at the newspaper offices, to the City to discover the Wren churches and to attend recitals of Bach fugues, to wicked Soho, and down to the Docks.

These were the last years of his boyhood, and though he felt he must escape abroad to find his real true self, nobody describes better than he what it felt like to discover his city.

'London was not a city; it was a foreign country as strange as India. Often I longed to be in love; but I was already in love with London . . . a London of my own was seeping into me without my knowing it.'

CHAPTER NINE

Dame Edith Evans
Pimlico

'I'm not a go-backer, you know,' said Dame Edith Evans. 'I live for the present.' She had agreed with the greatest reluctance to make a return visit to Pimlico, where she was born and brought up, insisting that she remembered nothing, that she wouldn't recognize anything, that it was all too long ago.

'I know I'm disagreeable and horrid,' she kept saying, 'but I'm doing what I dislike most. I never look back on my life. I don't know what I was doing at forty! That's why I don't look as old as I am. *I'm* not interested in my age, it's everybody else who is.'

Dame Edith's interesting age is eighty-six, and it is true that she doesn't look it, with her black cap and her stunning long slim legs. 'My legs are not pretty: they are straight,' she says. 'That, at my age, is something to be grateful for. No bumps and bits and pieces. I am glad my legs aren't bumpy.'

'They kept telling me it is nine years since I was on the stage. Nine years! But I certainly haven't been sitting on my fanny for nine years, doing nothing, I'd have been bored stiff! I must have been abroad or something, doing films.'

Every word, as always, is enunciated in those unmistakable emphatic tones. 'I *think* I was born in Ebury Square,' she said vaguely. 'And then we lived in Ebury Buildings – in those days we weren't too proud to call them Buildings and then in Ebury Street. I was very *Ebury*.

'I may not have been well-born, but I was very *well-bred*. My mother was a woman of great energy, and she wanted something to do, so my father took a lodging-house, what was then called a lodging-house, in Ebury Street. For the gentry, just two couples at a time, people coming up to Court, as it was called. And it was a great success.'

This was at 109 Ebury Street, one of the more kempt and pretty, white-fronted Georgian houses at what Lady Bracknell would have called the right end of the street. 'Well, a hundred and nine, bless you!' cried Dame Edith on seeing it.

Next door lived Noel Coward and his family, though the untheatrical Evanses were not to know this, and at No 121 lived George Moore, the Anglo-Irish man of letters who was the first to notice the young Edith Evans.

What she remembered best about Ebury Street was the butcher just round the corner, Mr Francis (it is still called P. Francis and Son though it has changed hands) where she would be sent for her mother's meat.

'Everything was very personal. He wouldn't let me take anything that wasn't absolutely splendid. He would say, "Oh, no Edie, I can't let you have that, your mother wouldn't like that." Because we didn't have Common Things and we didn't do Common Things.'

She says she was a maddening child. 'I drove my parents crazy. Well of course I didn't have a theatrical background and they didn't know what to do with all my *energy*. I sent them off their chump.' So when she became an actress, 'It was an entirely new life, yet I knew that it was where I wanted to be. I had felt a bit of an odd fish before, I never knew what I wanted to do, I had no ambition.'

Her father was a civil servant and a Westminster City councillor. 'He worked in the Post Office and went as high as he could go, until he was sixty, when he retired and bought a house at Eastbourne.'

Her mother and father were devoted, and Edith, an only daughter, lived at home with them until she was thirty-five, even after her marriage. Since her mother always cooked for her, Dame Edith is just learning to cook now.

She left her local school, St Michael's, just before she was fifteen and was apprenticed to a milliner in Buckingham Palace Road for two years. She still has the indenture somewhere. 'I couldn't make dresses because long sleeves bored me, but I loved handling all the lovely materials and I loved the other girls.'

The establishment was at the Gorringe's end of Buckingham Palace Road, run by a Mr Blackaller. 'Rather a handsome man, but he put the fear of God into me. The millinery department was run by a Mrs Tanner, and if we wanted a favour we would put her shoes on for her. Sometimes we would put them on still stuffed with paper – oh, we had all sorts of larks.'

After Blackaller's there were other millineries, all around the Victoria area. 'That's where I fell through the roof,' she pointed out to us as we passed Hobart Place. 'I'd been locked in the work-room during the lunch-

Ebury Street: 'It's not my London any more'

hour, so I climbed through a window and tried to walk over a roof that I thought was tin. It looked like tin to me. But it was in fact glass, and I fell through it. They were livid with me! They felt I had no business falling through their roof. They even made me pay for a glass of milk I had spilt. You see I was always making a disturbance and fuss.'

She was busy and boisterous: 'I remember being astonished once when Jack Hawkins told me his children were always asking, "What can we do now, daddy?" I was occupied the whole time! Never had a minute!

'When I came home in the evening my mother would hand me a silver tray and a white apron and I would have to take up dinner for the guests, and then I would run across Ebury Bridge to my night school. To Shake-speare.'

This was a drama class run by 'my dear Nell Massey', which later developed into the Streatham Shakespeare Players, who did a Shakespeare production every year. Through this, Edith Evans was discovered, in her twenties, in the classic manner: William Poel of the Elizabethan Stage

Society saw her playing Beatrice and asked her to come and act for him.

This is how she came to play Cressida at the King's Hall, Covent Garden – where George Moore spotted her – in the evenings after working on the hats all day.

'Dear William Poel took me straight to the heart of the West End, where everybody spoke so beautifully, Mary Jerrold and Hubert Harben, and I picked up everything from them. I've more or less always spoken Beautiful English.'

And were her parents proud of her then? 'No, not at all! They didn't believe in pride, in our house. If you did it you did it, that was that. If people praised me in front of me, said how good I was in a play, my mother would say, "I thought they were *all* very good." She wouldn't have me picked out: that was bad manners.

'Mother was not the sort of person who gave unnecessary praise. I was never told I had any good qualities. She once told me, as a child, "You have pretty hair and nice hands, but the rest . . ." I thought I was a very plain girl and I said to myself, Oh all right I shall enjoy myself anyway. It didn't upset me, I had a good time because I was a pretty larky girl.'

It was at the drama classes that she met her future husband, George Booth. 'He came along with a friend who liked acting. We used to go cycling very early in the morning, he and I, to Richmond Park.'

But it was not until some years later that Miss Evans 'dwindled into a wife'. He went abroad, and she was on the stage. He was a petroleum engineer, and when they did marry, at she-can't-remember-which church in Pimlico, while she was playing Portia at the Old Vic, he went abroad again immediately. It was a year before anybody realized she was married and then the beastly Press wanted to know all about it.

'It is not,' declared Edith Evans at the time, 'of the slightest interest to anyone except myself to know to whom I am married.'

Buckingham Palace Road is largely unrecognizable to her, with its monuments to air travel and its domination by British Airways and Pan-Am signs. Even the relics of her day are under threat: the ornate late-Victorian Public Baths and Library are closed and scheduled to be re-developed. '*My* library,' she recalled. 'Oh, how I longed to get books from there! But I wasn't old enough: you had to be ten to join. I remember going along, and the librarian saying "How old are you, dear?" and I whispered, "Nine", hoping he wouldn't hear.'

Passing St Gabriel's, Warwick Square, the church where she sang in the choir, we went to Claverton Street, where the family lived for many years, the house she was married from. Most of Claverton Street exists no more, and what is there is woefully crumbly and decrepit, but her house is still

55

there, No 17, with lots of bright yellow window-boxes on top of its heavily pillared porch.

The look of the entire street is utterly changed. 'But of course it's years ago, heavens above, ancient history.' To the right used to be the Army Clothing Stores; now it is the back of Dolphin Square. And across the road directly are the glass pyramids of the Pimlico Comprehensive School, where a passer-by tells us thousands of children fry each summer.

Dame Edith looked almost as dismayed by the look of the street as by the experience of being photographed. 'I Am A Woman Who Has Always Disliked Being Photographed,' she said. 'I never do it gracefully. Can't be happy! Can't! Hate it!'

A lifelong Londoner, she has now exiled herself to the country, to a beautiful Tudor house in Kent. 'I come up occasionally,' she says, 'to see my dentist or the optician; and whenever I gather a little money together I go to my dressmaker at Hardy Amies (there is one dressmaker who works only for the Queen and me) only that is so terribly expensive now. Who can afford it? I can only suppose gangsters' molls!

'I lived in Albany thirty years, you know, and that was very nice, but once you stepped into Piccadilly it was horrid. I would never want to live in *this* London again' – waving an imperious arm down Claverton Street – 'it's not *my* London, it's not *my* Piccadilly. Not any more. And I wouldn't know how to find my way about!'

CHAPTER TEN

Harry and Bob Harris
Bankside

Harry Harris was a famous old Southwark lighterman. One of the sixth generation of Harrises to take to the water, he wished his forefathers had recorded something about their lives – so he did himself, in 1935, writing a graphic memoir of river life that the family has kept.

Harry Harris knew that his way of life would not survive for long. 'Don't be a tug skipper,' he said to his eldest son, Harry. But his youngest son, Bob, went ahead: he was apprenticed to his father in 1936, was a tug skipper for twelve years, and is now a journeyman lighterman for Thames and General Lighterage.

The best way to see the river is from the river, so we hired a motor launch and took a trip – Harry junior, now sixty-seven, and brother Bob fifty-five – on the waterway they know so well. Typically, Bob brought along his grubby 1954 *River Thames Wharf Directory*, published by Gaselee and Son, the old family towing firm he once worked for.

We embarked at Cherry Garden Pier, Rotherhithe. The two brothers are born sailors: they remembered going down the river in their grandfather's boat, the Jubilee, as soon as they could walk. 'Father always wanted us to love the river,' they say. 'He had all the river skills and knowledge, and was completely fulfilled exercising them.'

A man of contentment and much dignity (it's clear from his memoirs) he passed on his skills and knowledge to his sons. So they knew, when we set off, when the tide would have risen; they could point out which bridges are 'a straight run through' and which have deceptive tidal sets; they could count the stones visible above the water on Blackfriars Bridge and know if there was enough height to berth barges.

The Thames is an incomparable river, with all its dramatic associations – Execution Dock, where Captain Kidd hanged; Limehouse Reach and

'And now this great God-given highway has been allowed to die'

Chinatown; Traitor's Gate; Wapping Old Stairs where the Hanging Judge Jeffreys was trapped in an inn while on the run. Memories and thrilling bits of history linger in each name, but our little motor launch had a lonely ride. For the river, as all watermen and lightermen agree, is dead, compared with what it once was.

There was the odd hovercraft, tourist boat, river police launch. And a couple of tugs with barges: the Messina, from Mercantile Lighterage, bearing about two thousand tons of sugar from Dagenham to Hammersmith; the General VII, from Thames and General, carrying six tea craft from Tilbury to Brentford. But only a few years ago there would have been dozens of such tugs and barges in and out of the wharves all the time.

'Only six years ago the few wharves at Bankside that remained from the original thirty-two were moving 150,000 tons of cargo a year,' recalled Bob. 'And now this great God-given east–west highway has been allowed to die.

'These tugs tow six barges each with two thousand tons – twelve hundred tons of copper or grain or tobacco or sugar or coffee or tea, with no traffic lights, no congestion, no juggernauts, no exhaust fumes, no noise! Think of the saving in fuel! America has realized the truth, and doubled the amount of cargo carried on rivers in the last ten years. The Common Market countries rely heavily on waterway traffic. It doesn't make sense.'

The London Dock, built in 1800–5 by Asher Alexander, architect of Dartmoor, is an empty basin. St Katharine's Dock has become a smart marina for the wealthy.

Of the wharves, only the names remain, emblazoned proudly like that of Ozymandias above what are now derelict and blind-windowed prison-like warehouses. Some have a majestic beauty – Hay's Wharf, for instance, and the luxuriously redeveloped Oliver's Wharf at Wapping – but now, without the river life around them to give them character and purpose, they rise sheer and bleakly deserted from the river.

'You've got to have change. But why change the good things? You could still carry goods up river to Blackfriars Rail Wharf, now derelict, and shift it to the railway to go all over the country.

'I'm very keen on a new society, that's been formed, called ToW – Transport on Water. And I'm sure if my father were alive he'd feel the same as I do,' says Bob.

'He would only agree to one of us being apprenticed, it's true. But at the same time he was sure that there would always be trade on the river. When I took off and went farming for a bit, he was mad at me.'

Old Harry Harris was born in 1880 in Park Street, Southwark. He wasn't supposed to roam around Bankside, Southwark's waterfront, formerly known as the notorious Stewes. But he soon learned every inch of the bank, swam in the river, knew where to hide when the tide was out, and where to climb ashore other than the landing stairs. He was, he wrote, completely at home in and on the water.

The scenes described in his memoirs will never, alas, be seen again on the Thames and they have enormous vitality and colour. In 1887, Queen Victoria's jubilee, the entire Harris family celebrated by rowing to Richmond and back, marvelling at the grand houses and waving trees at Putney.

In 1894 young Harry, just apprenticed to his father at twelve shillings a week, was the boat boy at the opening of the gaunt Gothic Tower Bridge by the Prince of Wales. And in the same year there was a bitterly cold winter and the river became unnavigable because of the ice. The Thames didn't freeze but snow from the streets was dumped there, forming ice floes that stuck to the bottoms of the barges.

In 1903 and 1904 he went swan upping, rowing from Southwark Bridge to Marsh Lock at Henley, to mark and pinion the young cygnets. He rowed stroke oar in the King's boat. Then, rowing was vitally important: Harry took immense pride in his skill with an oar of any size up to thirty foot, and wrote in his memoirs: 'Even today (1935), to see a youth cuddling an oar when handling makes one feel similar to a drill sergeant watching an awkward squad.'

The watermen have always been a clannish fraternity, known as Down Towners who despised the landsmen or 'linen drapers'. The river was 'the ditch', bridge arches 'holes', oars 'paddles'.

'Every waterman has a nickname,' wrote old Harry. 'Tubby, Podge, Narrow, Rasher, Dub-Toe, Winkle-eye, Little Biggie, Knicker, Knacker, Knocker, Walloper, Masher, Rum and Rags, Dosey, Slowman and Squibs. Every Perkins became Polly and every Robinson Cockie.' Harry's brother Charlie, tugmaster at Gaselee's, was known as Scratcher because he would always sound the river, find the depth of water under him.

All the watermen went regularly to the riverside music-halls, the Old Vic and Gatti's in the Westminster Bridge Road. Harry Harris recalled the Relief of Mafeking being announced from the stage on a Friday night at Gatti's.

'Kate Carney, the coster singer, emptied the house by announcing the news. Pubs closed at 12.30 in those days, but had to close earlier that night because their stocks ran out. London went crazy.'

Just as we were approaching the rungs of the ladder to climb ashore at Bankside, our boat got a rope tangled in its propeller. 'The old-fashioned rope, made of natural fibres, would sink,' Harry Jnr explained. 'The modern plastic rope floats, and this is what happens.'

It was time to go ashore because, as Harry told me with much solemnity, 'Part of the art of lightering is to know the time of the tides. And the times of the opening hours.' Certainly, the pubs are nowadays the liveliest parts of river life: the Anchor, the Mayflower, the Angel, the Prospect of Whitby, all thrive on the riverbanks even though the river trade has dwindled so.

Though, as their abstemious father said in his memoirs, recalling how some lightermen would tap their casks of wine, rum and gin, 'Abstainers and temperate men were the best friends for a lad, they were neater, cleaner and kinder.' One night as an apprentice he went to work with a drunkard who was later found drowned. 'Without being gruesome,' he said, 'dead 'uns were common sights to the riverside.'

Both he and his father were swept overboard; but the Harrises are survivors, as a family. Bob Harris never feared the water even after he fell into a stream at the age of two and lost all his hair for ever. 'We tried everything: bear's grease, paraffin, but it never would grow again.

'Our life as children was lived around the tides,' said Bob. 'You knew when your father would be home, or not, according to the tides. And Dad had the knowledge of all the tides and bridge sets.

'Vauxhall Bridge, for instance. Very tricky. For the first two hours of the ebb, the tide sets hard to south'ard. After that it's a straight shoot through. Later on the water comes back and at the last of the ebb you get a slight set to the nor'ard. So at Vauxhall Bridge you have to know how to position yourself. You can do a lot of damage with three hundred feet of barges, if you have six of them in tow. Oh, Dad could talk about this sort of thing for hours. And I would appreciate his knowledge, as a tug skipper.'

It will be a sad day when there are no more Harrises on the river. Their family tree is traceable back to the Great Fire, and always around Southwark.

Today, there are only twelve hundred lightermen, and only a dozen or so are apprenticed each year. 'Dad could see that the trade was shrinking,' says Bob. 'And he was a bit concerned that he'd done wrong by putting me into it. But I reassured him. I thanked him. It was a marvellous life.'

CHAPTER ELEVEN

Daphne Fielding
Belgravia

Some generations belong precisely to their time and place: New York in the twenties had the perfect antidote to Prohibition in Scott-Fitzgerald's Jazz Age people; London at the same time had its ideal equivalent, the Bright Young Things.

Daphne, daughter of Lord and Lady Vivian, was one of the brightest: high-spirited, exuberant and witty. So beautiful that her brother would hire out her photograph for a shilling a time at Eton, she wore flapperish cloche hats, dazzled the débutante circuit of the London Season, and married the Marquess of Bath.

She was born in 1904, in her grandmother's house at 11 St James' Square, practically next door to the London Library, 'which has become one's lifeline, living abroad: I use it all the time'.

The family home was at 20 South Eaton Place: Belgravia at its most handsome, consistent and bland. Cream stucco façades, imposing pillars and black wrought-iron balconies and railings as far as the eye can see. Timeless and unchanging.

When Daphne was just four, and her brother Tony three, her mother left her father.

'My mother married four times,' she says, 'and might have married a fifth, had she not found out that the man for whom she had left my father already had a wife.

'My dearest memory is of my father and mother having a tremendous row, shouting at each other – it was something to do with a snaky watch chain she'd given him. I remember a maid picking me up, and she was wearing a navy blue and white spotted blouse with leg o' mutton sleeves, and because I was so terribly frightened of all the noise, I hid my face in her sleeve.

The Peter Pan statue in Kensington Gardens: 'so very Arthur Rackham, this tree'

'My mother was a very temperamental woman, and after she left us she went on the stage. She did Pelleas and Mélisande at the Lyceum, which according to my grandmother was a very vulgar theatre.

'In those days divorces were so different. One's mother's name was never mentioned, and one intrigued to find out about her. One glamourized her. I didn't see her until I married Henry Bath, and we bicycled out to Switzerland to visit her.

'So all my early outings and jaunts, endless lovely treats, were with my two grandmothers, who were totally different and hated each other.

'One was the widow of Henry MacCalmont, whose racehorse Jerry M won the National; and the other was a grand old lady, the Dowager Lady Vivian, who had been ambassadress in Rome. I loved her.'

Meanwhile, at home, a succession of ladies were invited to lunch with Lord Vivian, handsome and eligible. 'We always twigged, even as children, the ones who were after him, because they were terribly nice to us, and gave us chocolates and huge dolls.

'Then he married my angelic stepmother: we were frightfully lucky. She had been widowed at nineteen. Her husband died on the honeymoon. So she was still in half-mourning, and didn't bring us presents, but she was the first person who read *Alice In Wonderland* to me, and always throughout life guided my reading.'

A series of unfortunate governesses came and went, finding the two children ungovernable.

'I remember my father, who was in the 17th Lancers, was often chosen to be cotillon leader at dances, and he would bring us back the favours he had been given. One was an emerald green Frog Footman mask, and it just shows how little control our governess must have had: I insisted on wearing this frog mask for our walk in the park, with a blue felt hat on top.'

She grew up among distinguished and faintly eccentric relatives. 'I had twin aunts who were both maids of honour to Queen Victoria: Doris, who married Douglas Haig, the general, and Violet, who never married.'

Violet walked in a permanent aroma of exotic perfume. Prince Dimitri of Russia could always track her from one room to another at Sandringham by following the trace of her scent on the cushions.

Favourite childhood outings were to the Albert Memorial, which she adored; to Madame Tussaud's where her father would pretend to be a waxwork in the Chamber of Horrors and give people terrible frights by crying out; and to the Peter Pan statue in Kensington Gardens.

To Peter Pan we went again. 'It's so very Arthur Rackham, this tree,' said Daphne Fielding, burnishing with her gloved hand the bronze petal cap of one of the fairies. 'I remember being especially fascinated by the rabbits and the mice on the tree trunk.'

Then in her early teens her father sold the London house and they moved to Cornwall, being a Cornish family. But they continued to take a London house for the Season: large houses around Hyde Park, where they could have dinner parties for twenty people before dances, and where the rent was never above fifteen guineas a week. 'You'll have to get married soon, I'm not going to go on doing this,' her father told her.

They brought with them from Cornwall 'our dilapidated staff. A Cornish maid, a footman and a butler: my father favoured butlers who had been in the British Legion, so they were usually maimed or shell-shocked.'

To be a young débutante in the twenties was to engage in the single-minded pursuit of fun. Daphne (she adored the name; 'so chaste, and chased by Apollo, and turned into a tree') wanted to look like a Michael

Arlen heroine, and probably succeeded: a greyhound girl, tall and leggy, streamlined and hipless, breasts strapped down with constricting bodices.

'The actress I most wanted to emulate was Pearl White in *The Perils of Pauline*; I wanted my life to be like hers, perilous adventures and romantic rescues.' She did her best: life was a ceaseless round of forbidden diversions. 'There was so much forbidden territory that we explored it all the time: it was a challenge.'

She was not allowed to smoke, so she smoked through a long ivory holder, pretty Silver Crest cigarettes, or cigarettes with crimson rose-petalled tips given by a boyfriend – presents from boyfriends being also forbidden.

'We were never allowed to go to a party without a chaperone, my aunt Lady Worsley, or Lady Listowel, but we always managed to escape somehow: the chaperones got fed up sitting up so late, and we could always get door keys copied, go home and then creep out later and meet people under the Marble Arch.

'Then we would go to the Blue Lagoon, where a pianist played on the balcony, and we sang a song called Eat More Fruit: "Eve said to Adam, the cheeky little madam, Eat More Fruit."'

The most forbidden place of all, and therefore the most frequented, was the Cavendish Hotel in Jermyn Street, where the outrageous Rosa Lewis presided. Rosa Lewis had been Mrs Fielding's grandmother's cook once: why was her establishment so very wicked?

'Well, there was lots of gossip about her. Drinks after hours, and private sitting-rooms for her favourites, that sort of thing. And then there were her stays, which were supposed to be autographed by Edward VII. I saw them once; they were always figuring in fashionable treasure hunts, as objects to be secured. And she would wear what she called her "sables of sin" . . . she'd been a bit of a girl in her time. We'd go there in the afternoons, to escape from parties.'

On one occasion when she and her friends were staying with the Guinnesses in Ireland, they decided to dress up as highwaymen on their horses and demand money from passers-by. This had sorry consequences for Daphne: the old Lord Bath disapproved so strongly of this escapade that he forbade his son to see Daphne. So they had to meet in secret at the houses of friends.

Eventually they married in secret, at St Paul's Knightsbridge, with only two friends present; though they used their real names, nobody noticed, and the bridegroom went off to Texas while the bride stayed at home wearing her ring on a chain around her neck. Afterwards when both sets of parents relented and they were officially and publicly married in St

Martin-in-the-Fields, it was a much grander occasion with ten bridesmaids and four pages and a train-carrier.

The only problem, as Lord and Lady Bath discovered decades later when they were divorced, is that if you marry twice you have to divorce twice. They remain the best of friends: Lord Bath is now married to Virginia, niece of Iris Tree, who gave Daphne Fielding considerable help with her biography of Iris.

Today, Daphne Fielding continues to write her sparkling books and is rather sheepish about all those jolly pranks of her chums in the twenties. But what impresses most, in retrospect, is their harmlessness.

'There was one utterly silly thing that we used to do. There was a very disapproving, stuffy old dowager, the Dowager Lady Powis, who wore a diamond dog-collar and tiara and lived in Pont Street – we used to describe anything stuffy as "very Pont Street". On our way home from dances, we would gather outside Powis House and chorus "Goodnight Lady Po-Po-Po-Po-Powis!" Very innocent, I suppose, but *what* a bore for Lady Powis.'

CHAPTER TWELVE

Cissy Doyle
Piccadilly

Cissy Doyle, *née* Cicely Golden, had the stateliest of homes. From the age of four she was brought up in Burlington House, home of the Royal Academy in Piccadilly, where her father was head steward and her mother housekeeper for thirty-seven years.

She has remained a West End girl ever since: barely moving outside W1, working in every West End theatre, as a chorus-girl or in the box-office, and still living in the heart of Covent Garden theatreland.

Now, in her dramatic emerald-green fur-trimmed midi coat and high boots it is impossible to believe she will be eighty-six in March. People always did tell her she looked like Cicely Courtneidge.

'The West End is my life,' she says. 'I was spoiled. I never liked going over the water. I was only over the water once in my life.' By this she means across the river in Kennington, where she lived during the war. She finds it odd that she was happy there: 'It was the comradeship of those Lambeth Walk women with their coarse aprons. I'd never have met them otherwise.'

For the last thirty-eight years she has been at the Haymarket Theatre, doing any job that needs doing, but usually making herself hoarse telling visiting Americans about the history of the theatre. She has her own chocolate stall there. 'My family has often been connected with the Royalty,' she says.

'On Sunday afternoons my mother would prepare the Royal teas at the Academy; one day the Duke of Windsor and Princess Mary were running about in the gallery and Princess Mary was in a beautiful straw hat, and having a love of millinery I joined them, running round. I was made to go to bed for the rest of the day.'

She often goes back to the Royal Academy to look round, and we went

Burlington House: the stateliest of homes

there again together. She pointed to the flagstaff on the Burlington House roof. 'I must have had a nerve of iron,' she says, 'but when I was nine or ten I climbed that very flagstaff and slid down it. I was such a climber my mother had to nail up the windows. Makes me nervous just to look up there now.'

She learned to ride her bicycle around the courtyard. She was forbidden to cycle in Piccadilly, but she joined a cycling club called the Fireflies that met in Whitcomb Street, and would cycle down St James' Street into Hyde Park and around the Serpentine.

The Golden family lived in the household staff area, underneath the main entrance to Burlington House, and slept right up in the attic. 'There were ninety steps to climb. I've always had steps. In Maiden Lane now I have sixty-eight, and at the Haymarket Theatre a hundred and two if I go down to the bowels of the earth. But see how slim it keeps me.'

On the enormous kitchen range in the basement her industrious mother, a châtelaine with innumerable keys hanging on her apron, would cook for the Royal Academicians. All the members would say they never got coffee anywhere as good as Mrs Golden's. And Cissy did the shopping, in Duke Street and Jermyn Street at Robert Jackson (whisky 3s 6d) and of course at Fortnum and Mason. Piccadilly was her local High Street, Burlington Arcade her corner shops. 'We did eat well,' she says, 'because we ate what the members ate. I often think the stamina I have now comes from what I ate then.'

The Academy doesn't alter, and neither does its neighbour, the Society of Antiquaries, where Cissy recognizes the clock by Benjamin Gray and Justin Vulliamy in the hallway. Opposite, she says the Piccadilly Arcade used to be a music-hall where she would watch the magic shows of Maskalyn and Devant. And the next arched doorway to the Academy, up Piccadilly, is the door to Cut-Throat Lane, she says. 'Because all the young painters would bring their paintings by this door, and would despair when they were rejected.'

She went to school in Mayfair, at St George's, where she remembers once hopping on to the rail of a four-wheeler to be driven to school instead of walking, with her friend who was the daughter of the police inspector in Vigo Street. 'And Miss Farley, who had a nose like a parrot, brought us in front of the class saying: "Fancy, have you heard, these girls were hanging on the back of a milk-cart!" And I corrected her because it was a four-wheeler, not a milk-cart, and Essie and I laughed and laughed.'

Leaving school at fourteen, she got a job in a milliner's shop in Bond Street, while her sister Nellie went to a dressmaker in Albemarle Street. 'I must have been ambitious. I moved from one milliner at 2*s* 6*d* a week to another at 5*s* a week. And the milliner used to have her periods once a month and then I would manage the shop and get 8*s*.

'I had lovely golden hair right down to my waist, but I had it cut off specially to be a model for the hats.' In 1914 she was chosen to be one of the four girls selling chocolates in the box tier at the New London Opera House because of her hair (there were queues of girls after the job, stretching all the way down the Strand). And the Baron Rothschild would give her a golden sovereign every week: she saved forty of them.

This seems to have been nothing new to the golden-haired and thrifty Cissy. In her schooldays an elderly gentleman used to give her sixpence every week when she passed by, and she religiously took it to the St James' Place post-office every Saturday, even though her mother told her she mustn't take money from strangers.

She was married in 1925 in beautiful St James' Church, Piccadilly, built by Wren, consecrated 1684. 'I'm so glad it's been restored,' she says as we walk there. 'I couldn't believe it, that morning in 1940 when I saw what the bomb had done. I rushed straight over there when I heard. That was my sad day.

'In summer time, between shows, I go and sit in the gardens, they've made them so pretty.' We go inside to see the Grinling Gibbons carvings: 'There was no altar anywhere in England more handsomely adorned,' wrote John Evelyn in his Diary.

'I got to know Leopold Stokowski well here,' Cissy says. 'He used to conduct the choir and play the organ for us. He's a wonderful man. Last time I saw a picture of him I thought, you're getting on. But I suppose I'm getting on too.'

As we walk up Piccadilly, Cissy remembers it much more lavishly decorated for Christmas. But Fortnum's looks festive enough, and she wanders nostalgically among the pâtés and guava jelly and Périgord pies and truffles and Carlsbad plums. 'This shop has just the atmosphere that I love. Oh, the workmanship everywhere. "Now, don't forget your list, Cissy," my mother would say.'

She has a fine time too in Burlington Arcade, so preciously enshrining the exclusive purveyors of the best leather and china and tweed and silver and tobacco and finest linen. Since many of them have lived more than a century there, much remains the same; Cissy declares that Church's the shoemakers and Barnett the jeweller and Hummel's with the dolls look exactly the same, exclaims at the glittery parvenus like Ken Lane, and is glad to see the porters still in uniform.

Behind Burlington House we walk along Vigo Street to No 8 where Cissy used to go to tea, down in the basement which is now just a mass of rubble. Around is the usual mixture of careful preservation and ruthless change: above is a site acquired on behalf of Bangladesh Biman Airways; opposite stands Hawkes the tailor, two hundred years of service.

In Sackville Street around the corner from her childhood home Cissy lived later in life, on the fourth floor above what is now Austin Reed, next door to Hungarian Airlines.

'I opened up a little dress agency here when I had my hubby in hospital,' she says. 'And all the girls from the West End used to come here after their shows.' She still makes exquisite dressed dolls, with quantities of gold lace and velvet. 'I rake around the bin outside Bermans, and hope nobody's looking. They laugh at me at the theatre. Oh, Cissy, you don't go rag-picking? they say. But I do.'

Opposite, at No 32 Sackville Street, Hankey Bannisters is still, where Cissy bought wine for Academy dinners. Then she would watch from behind a screen in the banqueting hall, not breathing a word. 'I remember hearing that young prince speak, David that became George VI, and I thought what an ordeal for the poor boy, he stuttered so, and he rushed away down the stairs afterwards.'

As a small child she watched the funeral cortège of Sir John Millais leaving the Royal Academy. 'I can see it now: the most wonderful funeral I ever saw. He was laid in state in one of the galleries and I got into trouble for picking up a bunch of flowers.' Cissy thinks there are no artists now to compare with the Victorians.

'There was a sculptor called Gilbert, the one that did Eros,' she says. 'He would come down to our apartment at nine in the morning and drink beer from the barrel and play the piano. My mother used to get disgusted. He sent me chalks and sandpaper but he told my father, "Please, Golden, don't let your daughter be an artist, she'll be in poverty all her days." He died in Paris, himself a pauper.'

Each year when the entries for the exhibition came in, Cissy would judge for herself which would be rejected and which hung. She would get nineteen out of twenty right. And in the Academy there is still a tapestry hanging that she worked on herself. 'My mother asked my aunt Kay, who was a housekeeper in Thurloe Square, to come and repair it because she was so good with her needles, and we laid it on a trestle and mended it with fine little stitches. Oh, days and days we worked on it: a work of art.'

Living in such an extraordinary place, in the very centre of London, her memories are all very special. Getting locked in the Academy strongroom among all the Academicians' silver, until her father rescued her. Being held up on her father's shoulder on Mafeking night, when there were free drinks for all around Piccadilly Circus. Watching Queen Victoria in her pony and chaise in Hyde Park. Going to Westminster Pier on Sunday mornings for honey cakes and hot milk straight from the cow. Watching the Zeppelin raids from the Academy roof.

'Sometimes when I see bits of my London crumbling around me I ask myself, have we really progressed?' says Cissy. 'Oh, my God, that's down, I think to myself. I never thought I'd live to see the day they pulled down the old gentlemen's club just by Charles II Street, opposite the Haymarket Theatre. That's where my father sat on a trunk at the age of nine, when he arrived in London for his first job as a page boy.

'I do have the loveliest memories. Sometimes I sit on a Sunday and get the pictures out and I think to myself. "There. It's wonderful to have had a background like that." '

71

CHAPTER THIRTEEN

Felix Aprahamian
Muswell Hill

Felix Aprahamian, the music critic, has lived all his sixty years in the shadow of Alexandra Palace. In his infancy it was still a PoW camp, in his childhood its park was his playground. In his teens he was showing parties of people around the innards of the great Henry Willis organ, at sixpence a time. In recent years he has been a leading light of the Alexandra Palace Arts Society, pressing for better use of the sprawling acres of halls.

'As a boy I fell in love with the organ. Imagine, to have the finest concert organ in Europe on my doorstep! It was already a legend; it had been silent for years. It was Father Henry Willis's finest organ, better than the Albert Hall one, and now I am hoping that Willis IV and V will restore it again. It is my great passion. I shall die happy if I see that organ restored.'

Alexandra Palace's magnificent bulk, crowning the North London skyline, is just a few brisk paces from Felix Aprahamian's front door in Methuen Park, Muswell Hill, a road of Edwardian red-brick semis. The Palace is one hundred and three years old this year and its unfortunate history has never quite lived up to its pre-eminent situation: it has seemed, from the time it burned to ashes on its seventeeth day of existence, doomed.

It was supposed to be a Palace for the People, North London's answer to Crystal Palace, whence the eye could roam 'far over green hills and rich woodland crests'; but despite its terraces and wooded walks, its grandiose Italianate elegance enclosed in monstrous solidity, its exotic galleries and arcades, it was a mismanaged venture. Everybody connected with it seemed to go bankrupt, and it closed down seven times before 1900.

Today this peeling mausoleum of Victorian aspiration (seven-acre building, two-hundred-acre park), which started out with a Drury Lane-sized theatre and a cricket ground bigger than Lord's, three lakes, a racecourse, conservatories crammed with flora and fauna from every corner of the Empire, still has its screwball selection of activities, including the roller-skating rink, the old time music-hall on Fridays, the ski-slopes, and, of course, the BBC's Open University in temporary occupation. And on the day we climbed the hill to the Palace, Felix Aprahamian sat in the Great Hall that was all decked out for one of the GLC concerts, the towering hundred-foot organ shell at the far end.

'Do you think they will ever, in our time, be able to afford to build anything like this again?' he challenges, waving an arm up to the vaulted domes of elegant ironwork. 'All down these aisles there used to be more-than-life-size plaster figures of all the kings and queens of England. I believe they're still down in the honeycombs of cellars below, where the wild cats roam: what a collector's item!'

To him it might all be Versailles. With a bit of imagination. 'Shouldn't society ladies, who would formerly have gone to Gunter's or Rumpel-meyer's be coming up here to take Earl Grey tea and scented macaroons and rhum babas on the terraces? Doesn't it deserve a resurgence of elegance?

'I shall never forget the great Handel festival of 1938, when hundreds of people milled around the Italian rose garden. If they brought a chef in, they could make a go of it. If this were in France, André Malraux would come here and say, let it be done!'

When he was a baby he would be wheeled up to see the caged peacock in the park, and would romp on the knoll of ancient yew-trees in the Grove, the oldest part of the Palace. By his teens, the organ had been repaired after the terrible damage wreaked during the armistice junketings, the Great Hall re-opened with an Olde Englysshe Fayre (where young Felix gave the guided tours around the organ pipes) and there were gas-lit Saturday night concerts, Sir Henry Wood conducting, where you could hear the young Bachhaus and Galli-Curci and Frieda Hempel.

Felix Aprahamian, as his name suggests, is of Armenian descent. 'My father was a carpet broker who inherited a dud carpet firm from Calouste Gulbenkian, the Anglo-Caucasian Carpet Company.

'Both my grandfathers were Nonconformist ministers; a maternal uncle reverted to the religion of his forefathers and became Archbishop of Smyrna. So though I may look like fifty thousand rabbis, I have the odour of Christian sanctity about me.' His parents married in Constantinople, had fled the Turks during the Armenian massacres and came to London. Installed in Crouch End by 1912, they shortly moved up to newer Muswell Hill.

'My mother adored music, and would attribute my gifts to her having

73

Alexandra Palace: a peeling mausoleum of Victorian aspiration

listened to the bands in Finsbury Park while she was carrying me.' But father insisted that Felix should follow him into the Mincing Lane brokerage, 'so I had an ignominious nine years as an office boy, clerk and secretary, attending the London Metal Exchange twice daily when copper was £38 a ton'. Still, he went nightly to concerts, standing at every Prom every night from 1931 to 1936.

'I started living at night, after posting the late letters at Fenchurch Street Post Office. It was the finest training a music critic could have.' And during the war he became concert director and touring manager of the London Philharmonic, taking the LPO on its blitz tours.

He reflects with amusement that when his parents came to Muswell Hill they were the only Armenians in the area, and now their house, which Felix has never thought of moving from, is one of the few in Methuen

Park that is still a single-family house. 'I have acquired the patina of an old resident,' he says.

His garden is the paramount example of what all suburban gardeners strive for, over the decades. He used to marvel at his father's addiction to pottering there, and now regards it as a haven, wandering out through the french door and arbour, from the music-room with its harpsichord and grand piano, for ten minutes, interlude in the shade and birdsong filled peace.

Exotic plants and trees abound; azaleas and camelias blossom at one side, roses climb the wall at the other; a cat called Tyger lopes through the irises; there is a bamboo summer-house for Japanese tea ceremonies, a hundred goldfish in the two ponds; a fountain, and a fifty-year-old vine clambering over the pergola.

'Just a suburban back yard, barely thirty feet by sixty,' he says, 'but it shows what can be done, and unlike my friends who live at Richmond and Ham and have far grander gardens, I don't have a jet screaming overhead every few minutes.'

It is a house filled with the accumulated paraphernalia of the music critic: whole sections of bookshelves on all the composers, signed portraits and photographs of singers and conductors, historic concert programmes, scores and sheet music. A librarian has to come in three times a week to sort and file. And the room known as the library started out as the infant Felix's nursery: bedroom, den, study, library, it has grown older along with him.

Still, he found it necessary to build another den in the roof, and from this room, if the plane trees were not so abundant, the view is straight over to Alexandra Palace.

Just by the window lies an Aeolian harp. 'If the wind were in the north you could hear its strange music. A beautiful sound. Like the wind in the telegraph wires, creating a turbulence: you hear the upper partials and harmonics.'

It pleases him to think that Elgar used to come to Muswell Hill and walk past his house, to visit Alfred Jaeger, Nimrod of the Enigma Variations, in nearby Rosebery Road. 'And Nimrod's widow used to take tea with my mother!' Aprahamian has a special love for Elgar, on whom he lectures. 'And imagine, I was put up for the Athenaeum by Sir Adrian Boult, who himself was put up by Elgar!'

Muswell Hill is, he believes, 'the most beautiful suburb in the world. It hasn't the elegant ostentation of Hampstead or Highgate perhaps, but it's got the old-fashioned personal shops still, like Martyn's the coffee shop where everybody seems to have all the time in the world. I regret the passing of Mr Cole the chemist, who was as good as a family doctor, prescribing remedies for everyone's spots and gumboils.

'There used to be a carriage and pair plying for hire in the courtyard of Muswell Hill Station. The whole family would pile in for excursions out to Shenley and South Mimms, to the great acres and the grand houses, with the coachman in his top hat.'

Muswell Hill Station? Alas, the old Broad Street line, running up to Alexandra Palace, when season-ticket holders wore toppers and spats on their way to the City. 'This branch of the Broad Street line was an artery, a lifeline, for Muswell Hill, and its loss was not only shortsighted, it was unpardonable,' roars Felix Aprahamian.

Inaccessible, but worth the journey: the views from the Palace grounds are stupendous, down to Blackheath and beyond to the North Downs, accompanied by the bracing wind that Felix Aprahamian says blows straight off the Urals and into his dining-room window. It could make his Aeolian harp sing like mad.

One can understand his emotional attachment to the place, as he gazes on the organ – ruined again in the Second World War, when the bombs fell and torrential rain poured in. At least the Great Hall has been used – Menuhin has conducted three Messiahs there, and such concerts will flourish if the Palace for the People has a future after all.

CHAPTER FOURTEEN

Louis Heren
Shadwell

Louis Heren, Deputy Editor of *The Times*, grew up in Shadwell, down by the London docks, where his widowed mother ran a coffee-shop called The City of Dublin Dining Rooms. It had emblazoned on the window the sign "A Good Pull Up for Carmen". Opposite, the men would line up for work at the West Garden Gate of the docks. 'Our mum used to watch to see how many men got work,' says Heren, 'to see how many dinners would sell that day.'

We took a walk around Shadwell to see what had become of Louis Heren's childhood home. When he was born in 1919, the shop stood next to the Lord Lovat pub on the corner of The Highway and Dellow Street, E1, opposite the stables and garage of the Meredith and Drew biscuit factory. There was life and activity everywhere.

Today Dellow Street is no more than a passageway between blocks of council flats: the Solander Gardens Estate. 'I know where they got that name,' says Louis Heren. 'The next street up was called Solander Street, but we always called it Polish Street because it was full of Polish Jews.'

No trace of any such ethnic distinction remains. In fact no trace of any distinction at all: one could hardly envisage a more lifeless scene. As we stood there, talking and watching, not a soul came or went, or called out, or even looked from a window. Only the occasional car came by.

It could not be more different from the 1920s Dellow Street that Heren describes so vividly in his book *Growing Up Poor In London* (a title his mother objected to: she thought it should be *Growing Up With The Poor*. Her great aim in life was to get the family out to the mecca of Bromley, Kent).

Then, Dellow Street was constantly noisy and alive. People put their kitchen chairs outside on the pavement in summer. The cobbles and the steel-rimmed cartwheels made it always noisy. But even on the verandah-walkways of the tenement blocks, people would be scurrying about all day. A seaman once told Heren it reminded him of Naples.

'Now, it could be a prison,' says Heren. 'It's as if a young architect were playing about with concrete for the first time. Brutal modern. I suppose they're nice flats inside.'

Alongside Mrs Heren's coffee-shop there used to be a row of cottages and shops. 'Mr Wolvewitch's bootshop, Mr Barron's sweets and ice-cream shop, and the Jewish food shop, where my mother got her kaese,' recalls Heren.

His conversation is peppered with references to the different races that abounded in Shadwell once, people who simply arrived by ship and stayed right there. His own mother, who was born in the Artichoke pub on the Whitechapel Road, was the daughter of a German from Frankfurt-am-Main; his father was the son of a French Basque, who got off the boat at St Katharine's Dock, found digs in Leman Street and stayed.

The first school Louis went to was right opposite their shop, the Highway School, where he was made to feel rather foolish in his Little Lord Fauntleroy suit. That school is gone (more Solander Gardens Estate) but his next school, a few hundred yards around the corner in Cable Street, is still there.

Here he wore a green blazer, played second violin in the school orchestra, was a contemporary of the present editor of the *Jewish Chronicle* (the school was two-thirds Jewish) and met the vital Miss Nixon, the English teacher who introduced him to Hemingway's writing. Little did she know that Louis Heren would be the man who, as a foreign correspondent, introduced Graham Greene to *the* Quiet American.

No longer is St George's School in Cable Street, a breeding-ground of fine upstanding citizens (it backs on to the lovely wild churchyard of St George's in the East, then, as now, a rare patch of greenery in the grey wastes). It is now the Nathaniel Heckford School for maladjusted children; and even the caretaker sorrowfully says the school has a pretty hopeless task. Only the other day one of the Georgian houses in Cable Street had been done over by a gang of boys from the school.

A walk along Cable Street produced many recollections. 'I wonder if poor kids nowadays depend on the library as much as we did,' said Heren as we came across Library Place. 'Here was the library.' And here was an empty space with a sign reading: 'New Amenity Open Space for Tower Hamlets.' Not even a bench to sit; one plant sprouting lamely in mid-concrete.

'This was a splendid library. A wonderful staircase, so you felt as if you

Watney Street: 'Life was always exciting and crowded'

were somewhere important. It was warm, and panelled, with green-shaded lamps, and matting on the floor, and of course, the books.

'A lot of Lascars, Indian seamen, married white women and lived along here. They were considered fallen women of course. But Cable Street was basically still quite respectable in my youth. If this house (pointing to one of the Georgian terraces) was in Hampstead, it would go for £80,000.'

We passed the old Town Hall, where the Heren family would gather on election nights to cheer the (inevitably Labour) victory. We passed the new swimming baths by St George's Church, where used to stand the Gunboat, a rowdy Irish pub, with a lodging-house for sailors known as a tuppenny rope – because they slept on hammocks instead of beds. 'We could always smell curry from the Sikh pedlars cooking in there,' says Heren.

'The thing about Shadwell,' said Heren, 'is that it was a riverside village hundreds of years before the urban sprawl. It was all tied up with the river, and the community was exactly the same as in a village. For one thing, everything was within walking distance. It was friendly, it was noisy and lively, and without being too nostalgic life was always exciting and crowded.'

Nearby, Watney Street could have remained what it always was, the most important shopping street in the area: it still has Shadwell Station (one of the earliest, on the Metropolitan line down to New Cross) where the young Louis used to put his blind Uncle Lou on the train to the Admiralty each morning. There was the unbroken line of market stalls and naphtha flares and noise of the stallholders' cries. But it is a shadow of its former self now.

The pitifully few shops that do remain in Watney Street from the old days are marvellous: crowded with a shambles of stock, looking flyblown and makeshift but somehow nevertheless reliable, like shops in rural Greece or North Africa. There's a nice old general store, L. Swaine, established 1910, remaining from Mr Heren's boyhood; and the Lord Nelson pub, with its elaborate sign for Burton Brewed Beer, stands on a corner.

But alas, the rest is just acreage of corrugated iron, boarding up what was once a life-force in the area. The old Sainsbury's, so important in bringing hygiene to shops, is boarded up at No 66. 'It was a marvellous place, where the butter was served from casks with a wooden spatula,' Heren recalls.

Everywhere are the signs of docklanders' fight for survival but in the face of such overwhelming changes in their environment it seems a hard struggle. 'FIGHT! Defend the football pitches taken from us by Council, Demo match Sunday Bigland Grass,' reads a poster on the door of the East London Family Service Unit, formerly the 'MD School' – school for the mentally deficient.

The only remaining member of Heren's family still living in the area is Mary O'Brien, an Irish Catholic servant who came to the family from an orphanage before Louis was born. She lived as family and later married the blind Uncle Lou, with whom she would go up West every Saturday night, to a movie and then a Lyons Corner House. 'They were great places in those days,' says Heren, 'the first places where East Enders would sit down to a table with a cloth on it.'

Finally we took a walk down to the river past the touristique Prospect of Whitby, a short walk away from the steps where the child Louis and friends used actually to dive into the soup-like River Thames. 'One day I dived in,' says Mr Heren, 'and I came up, spouting water, and opened my eyes to see a dead rat, yellow belly upwards, floating past. But it was still the best place to swim. It cost tuppence in the swimming pool.'

CHAPTER FIFTEEN

Kingsley Amis
Norbury

Kingsley Amis, the poet, novelist and critic, had an unpropitious upbringing in one of those South London suburbs that is barely distinguishable from any other: Norbury in the grey southern suburbs.

Norbury had, he warned me, always lacked identity. 'It wasn't like Streatham. At least Streatham had been a country town in the eighteenth century, where Dr Johnson would drive out to see Mrs Thrale for tea.

'Norbury was an artificially created place. It happened with the coming of the railway: the stretch between Streatham and Croydon was too long so they planted a station in between and called it after the only named building in the area, a house called Norbury Manor.'

We passed familiar childhood landmarks; Streatham Hill Theatre (now bingo); and the Gaumont, pronounced Gaumong, now a bowling alley, where you could get phosphates which were cheaper than ice-cream soda, in the balconied café. 'In that parade next to it were the Carlotta Tea Rooms. You can imagine what they were like. Very good doughnuts.'

We stopped at what looks like a sluggish ditch by the side of the Sussex Tavern and running under the High Road.

'This is The Brook,' said Amis, 'always known as The Brook. It runs up past the tennis club where my parents used to go; it comes in my book *The Riverside Villas Murder*.' It is, in fact, the River Graveney, as an old LCC notice informs us, exhorting us not to throw refuse on its banks.

In the Sussex Tavern he was delighted to find a notice-board for the local GRICE-hockey club, which he copied down in glee in his novelist's vade-mecum notebook ('It *must* be a combination of grass and ice') and he declared that now we were approaching Norbury he felt a Betjeman poem stirring within.

His family, the Amises and the Lucases, were firmly suburb-dwellers, Baptists of the Denmark Hill community. Father met mother in chapel where father played the organ. Grandfather, J. J. (John Joseph) Amis, was a glass merchant, doing fine until Woolworth's came along. Then Uncle Leslie (last heard of planning a cycling tour of Germany at the age of eighty-eight) had to carry on the business, downhill. The other uncle on that side was Uncle Pres (J. Preston) Amis, father of John Amis the music critic.

'And there was one sister, Auntie Gladys, forbidden by Pater, my unspeakable grandfather, to marry an American solely on the grounds that he was an American.'

Kingsley Amis was an only son. He was not called after Charles Kingsley, but after a cousin of his mother who was one of a pair of twins sweetly named Kingsley and Queenie. He fared better than his mother, who was named Rosa Annie after two aunts who both drank themselves to death. She preferred to call herself Peggy, a dashing, go-ahead name in those days.

The only man of letters in the family was mother's brother, George, a postman. But maternal grandfather, a shop assistant in Izaac Walton, the outfitters in Brixton, had all the English poets on his shelves and was the only literary influence in Amis's early life.

'It earned him a certain amount of obloquy, because he used to read Wordsworth out loud, and my grandmother would pull faces unkindly.

'My father was by no means a well-off man, underpaid throughout his life,' he said. 'He was a clerk in the export department of Colman's Mustard, in Cannon Street. Very publicity-conscious firm: you could belong to the Mustard Club and wear a badge. And when they moved to Norwich, father was left behind in the Bedford Square office. But he loved the City and talked endlessly about it.'

We visited the first two of the Amises' three Norbury homes. Each was of that distinctive but undistinguished suburban post-1918 pattern: three bed, two recep., the rooms small and boxy, but each house a mite more spacious than the last.

At No 14, Buckingham Gardens, the family home in 1922 when Kingsley was born, there now lives a family of six Jamaicans, the Lyseights, who were extremely jolly and welcoming. Mother, a nurse, was thrilled at the presence of K. Amis in her house: he must sign autographs for children Duane, Chris and Gary. A tablet on the living-room wall said: 'Christ the King is Head of This House – He Hears Every Word And Sees Every Act.'

Amis gazed out of the window across the square of identical plain little houses surrounding a green ('London Borough of Croydon: No Games Allowed on This Green' – why ever not?) and recalled the neighbouring

83

Ena Road, archetypally suburban: 3 bed., 2 recep.

families who lived there – 'Billy Mingo, Mrs Apps, the Coateses, and Mrs Nurser, who had no husband, which I found so interesting.'

'The smallness of 14 Buckingham Gardens, SW16, and of its successors,' he once wrote, 'was made mildly claustrophobic at times by my father's constant concern to prevent my getting away from him. . . . When I was at home, I kept finding that reading in public was deemed rude, while reading in private was anti-social. . . .

'The partition walls were not specially thick, and most sounds went through them. And the room where one was in the evenings was naturally the one with the wireless in it.

'Those who have grown up with the BBC Third Programme and Music Programme might find it difficult to imagine how music was broadcast in the thirties. One would go months without a chance to hear individual works . . . So I would very much want to listen to Brahms's Second Symphony any time it was available, and my father, after a day at the office and getting on for an hour's journey home, would very much not. And there we were.'

The auguries for a future Oxford scholar, Cambridge don and literary critic were not the most auspicious. He depended heavily on local libraries, the Tate Gallery and Queen's Hall concerts.

But there was music of a kind. 'My mother had a fine natural mezzo-soprano voice and would play the piano and sing those Victorian ballads with one-word titles like Because and Until. She was rather embittered because her sister Dora was the one chosen to have her voice trained.'

At the next house, 7 Ena Road, the end of a whitewashed terrace of four villas, Mrs Tant was not a bit surprised to see us. She knows the Amis connection because Panorama once photographed the house when they did Amis and Braine in a sort of Rags-to-Reactionaries programme.

In the back garden Kingsley said: 'See that tree stump? That was a bloody great oak tree. Immense tree, that.' It now has a red metal Jungle Gym suspended over it. 'We used to hang a cricket ball on a string from one of its boughs, and practise strokes.' Mrs Tant revealed that it was they who chopped down the tree, as it was diseased; it cost them £70.

Again Amis wandered round the house, locating where the wireless was (TV and stereo set now) and Patch's dog-basket and his desk in his bedroom. How little things have changed in Norbury, he remarked to Mrs Tant. 'Well,' she said, 'everyone tells us this area's come down such a lot. The golf course has been built over. You must have been here at the best time.'

We established that the Tant family exactly reflects the Amises in 1929: parents and one son, Paul, who is playing toy soldiers.

'Being an only child wasn't pleasant,' said Amis. 'This was a lower middle-class area, which meant you had to be very careful not to slip into the working class. And that meant that all friends brought home to tea had to be very carefully vetted. And that meant a great shortage of friends. My parents could not have restricted my choice of friends more assiduously.'

We took a walk up to the open space on Pollards Hill, which is pleasant and high and windy. The view is superb except for the tower blocks where there used to be fields as far as the eye could see. Kingsley used to fly model aeroplanes here; two little boys are flying ragged kites. Once more a sign says the playing of games is prohibited.

Then we sought another haunt: Norbury Library, a bright beacon in Beatrice Avenue, where Story Time was in progress, a group of children being read the tale of King Midas. Kingsley checked the titles of his own novels and found them all satisfactorily in the catalogue. But the Eng. Lit. section dismayed. 'Leo Rosten! Dorothy bloody Parker! What's she doing here?' And when he also found Alan Sillitoe and John Wain his voice reached a pained shriek. 'Used to have all the standard complete works. Where are the Complete Poems of Oliver Goldsmith? Oh, it's gone down.'

The most important influence in Amis's life was outside Norbury at the City of London School.

'Socially it was magnificent. I had a Church of England canon's son on one side and the son of a Stepney tailor, Jewish of course, on the other. And there was no snobbery whatever. Life at a large day-school in a large city embodies a freedom which I should guess to be unique.'

It is true that Norbury could not be more archetypally suburban: Kingsley winced at mock-Tudor and 'graveldash architecture where you put up wet cement and literally hurl gravel at it,' but was so taken with the shape of one gabled villa's pretty bay window that he urged me to make a sketch. Suburbia can provide such surprises.

The family stayed there until 1940, when Amis was eighteen, and it became clear that Norbury lay directly beneath the Germans' favourite bombing course. Father knew someone who lived in Berkhamsted, Herts, and took wife and son to stay there one weekend. The family never returned to Norbury.

Only once since then had Kingsley Amis been back – two summers ago when a visiting American academic expressed an interest. 'And I waited to see what I would feel: regret, nostalgia, misery, hope. But it was merely rather interesting, that's all.' This time he seemed greatly cheered by the experience. He didn't exactly say I Like It Here, but he chuckled all the time.

CHAPTER SIXTEEN

Sir Charles Tennyson
Regent's Park

For a man in his nineties Sir Charles Tennyson is incredible. A sprightly figure in black coat and hat, his mind sharp and observant; he laughs a lot and has a fund of good stories. Occasionally he will say 1832 instead of 1932, by mistake; the only reminder that he is a mid-Victorian.

He remembers his grandfather, Alfred Lord Tennyson, perfectly well. He has edited collections of the poet's works, and has written a book on Tennyson's correspondence with Queen Victoria, *Dear And Honoured Lady*.

'My grandfather was a very powerful personality. Very tall, strongly built, swarthy like a Spaniard with a long grizzly beard. He always wore these rather strange clothes, that long sleeveless Spanish cloak and that black felt wideawake hat, and he was very fond of walking his great dog.

'The last three years before he died when I was about twelve, in 1892, he seemed a rather remote and terrifying personality. He had had a very bad illness in the winter of '88–9, and it wasn't thought that he'd recover. He wasn't quite the same man afterwards and I think he was protected from all possible irritations.'

Sir Charles was born in 1879 in one of the finest Nash terraces in Regent's Park – Sussex Place. When we made our way through the park, past the magnificent white terraces on one hand and the vistas of green on the other, it seemed unbelievable that almost a century had passed since he lived there, leaving the Nash design mercifully so unspoiled.

Sir Charles was still thrilled by it all, exclaiming in delight at the little circular lodge at Hanover Gate, with the classical ladies in their Doric alcoves, and the Nash villas half-hidden among the trees.

But the way in which his home, in Sussex Place, has been preserved outside and utterly transformed inside was what astonished and pleased him

87

Sussex Place: an un-traditional Victorian childhood

most. The curving façade of Sussex Place is pure Nash, a sweeping two hundred yards punctuated by domed turrets. But on walking behind we discovered the completely modern building that is housed within – the London Business School, Sir Charles thought the transformation, which happened in 1968, very cleverly done.

We paid a visit to the double-turreted house at the southern wing of the terrace, which has been maintained exactly as it might have been, and is therefore most like Sir Charles's birthplace at No 5. It is the home of Professor Ball, principal of the London Business School.

'Ah! There's George IV. By Sir Thomas Lawrence, isn't it?' exclaimed the alert Sir Charles as he stepped into the drawing-room. The portrait, covering one wall of the immaculate Regency room, is on loan from the Brighton Pavilion. From the windows, the view is exactly as it was a century ago, over the lake.

In Sussex Mews at the back, all is modern: revolving doors into the school, and a driveway into a subterranean car park. Here used to be the stables and livery cottages in Sir Charles's day, though his family kept no carriage. 'It wasn't a terribly expensive house, I believe,' said Sir Charles.

'The last time I visited here was in 1909, when I married, and my wife and I came to dine with the Walter Leafs who lived in one of these houses.

Leaf was my godfather: he was chairman of Barclays Bank, but he also translated Homer, with Andrew Lang and F. W. H. Myers.

'My earliest recollection of Sussex Place is of going to have my portrait painted when I was not quite three. I went with my elder brother in a hansom cab, to an American lady, quite a good painter. And in the distance, from our hansom, we could see one of the great fires at Whiteley's store in Westbourne Grove. They had three fires, I believe.

'And while we were living here I saw what must have been one of the last surviving Jacks-in-the-Green, or Green Men, a survival from pagan times. A man dancing along the road in Regent's Park, dressed in leaves and flowers, playing on pipes.'

His recollections of his grandfather seem to be more vivid than those of his own father. Two things he remembers about his father. 'He used to wear a beard and moustaches, and I remember him twirling his moustaches and grinning like a cat, to amuse us.

'And on the staircase of the Sussex Place house was a photograph of a bust of Professor Adam Sedgwick who had been a friend of my father at Trinity. I remember asking my father, why was it called a bust? and he told me that Adam Sedgwick had bust and that was all that was left of him!'

Before we set out, Sir Charles had consulted a book called *Lionel Tennyson*, a life of his father. 'He seems to have died in India,' he said. 'In April '86. He was in the India Office, and the then Viceroy, Lord Dufferin, was a great friend of my grandfather, and invited my parents out to stay with him on a semi-official visit.

'They had a marvellous time and saw everything and my father did a lot of shooting which he enjoyed, but then he caught some fever, malaria I suppose, and he died on the voyage home. He was buried in the Red Sea.

'One of my grandfather's poems refers to it.' He found the poem in a volume of *Tennyson's Collected Works*, entitled 'To the Marquess of Dufferin and Ava', which includes the lines

> Your India was his Fate
> And drew him over sea to you.

and mentions 'your fatal shore' and 'that funereal boat'.

'We three sons had been sent to relatives in Scotland while my parents were away, and when we came home – I was about six – I shall never forget the sight of my mother, standing by a cane screen at the window of the dining-room at Sussex Place, in her widow's weeds, waiting for us.

'My mother was a very beautiful woman, the daughter of a very charming and delightful man named Locker, who wrote light verse and knew everyone in London. After the death of my grandmother Lady Charlotte Bruce, daughter of Lord Elgin, Mr Locker married a beautiful but not very intellectual American lady whose name was Lampson. So grandfather changed his name to Locker-Lampson.

'His new wife was only a few years older than my mother, and she proceeded to have four children, so these Locker-Lampson half-uncles were more like cousins.' I recalled the name of Locker-Lampson in connection with some jolly Edwardian practical joke.

'Oh yes,' said Sir Charles, 'that was their son Oliver Locker-Lampson, whose friend was the famous practical joker Horace de Vere Cole. One of his best-known hoaxes was that he dressed up as the Sultan of Zanzibar with his entourage, and pretended to have come to visit Trinity College, and fell down on his knees in Trinity Great Court before the Master. He also visited the Dreadnought impersonating the Emperor of Abyssinia's suite, with Virginia Woolf and Duncan Grant, to be received by Admiral May in full fig.

'But the joke he played on Oliver was that they were walking down Piccadilly one night, having dined rather well, and Horace de Vere Cole stopped to fasten a shoelace, and as Oliver walked on he suddenly ran after him shouting, "Stop, thief!" and accused him of stealing his watch. I think poor Oliver was an MP at the time, and there was a frightful fuss.

'Apparently de Vere Cole had been wounded in the South African war, and it was said this had affected his brain. He was a very entertaining fellow.'

After his father died Mrs Tennyson married Augustine Birrell. 'A very well-known man in his day, a delightful young barrister, born 1850, just beginning to make a name for himself as a writer of literary essays.

'When my mother married him we moved from Sussex Place to Albert Hall Mansions, overlooking Kensington Gardens. It was as far as I know one of the earliest mansion blocks in London, built in 1879 by Norman Shaw.' It is indeed one of the earliest such blocks, stylistically copied everywhere, with its arches and gables in many-coloured brick.

Most of his youth in Albert Hall Mansions he was away at school, at Eton. 'But I do remember sitting with my brother at our first-floor window with our pea-shooters, shooting at the people sitting on top of the horse-buses going west.

'My brother used to walk by himself across the park to a well-known school in Bayswater Road called Wilkinson's. Then both of us were sent to a boarding-school in the New Forest kept by a relative of the family called Rawnsley. It was convenient for the Isle of Wight where my Tennyson grandparents lived; we would go there for the summer, or to a house called Rowfant, near what is now the new town of Crawley, which belonged to Miss Lampson's father, a rich American engineer who took part in laying the first Atlantic cable and the South-Eastern Railway.

'Other children meant very little to me in my childhood. I was very close to my elder brother, less than a year older than me. We used to go sometimes to a sort of dome, what the devil were they called, in Westminster, where you stepped inside and it was like stepping into Venice. They were jolly good. And we would go to the panto to see eight-stone Dan Leno and twenty-stone Herbert Campbell as the Babes in the Wood, very funny they were too.

'I do want to stress,' added Sir Charles, 'that I had no experience at all of the traditional Victorian childhood. Neither from my own parents, nor from my stepfather and my half-uncles, did I have any sense of repression. Very much the reverse.

'In fact the Locker-Lampsons were the most notorious children, full of uproarious mischief. Once Augustine Birrell was sitting with Mr Locker in his library, which was supposed to be sacrosanct, and the four children suddenly burst in. Mr Locker turned to Mr Birrell and said, "Austin, think how terrible it would be if I had four children who made *no noise*." '

Sir Charles now lives in The Park, Hampstead, close to Anna Pavlova's house and the Waugh house on North End Road. 'It's a wonderful mess, old London,' he reflected as we went back home. 'Such a higgledy-piggledy of styles. But I must say I do like what they have done with Sussex Place. I think it's rather good.'

CHAPTER SEVENTEEN

John Herbert
Hammersmith

Boat Race Day is the day when all the enviable people with houses on the banks of the Thames are in their element. Perfect boating weather, the sun smiling on the magnolia trees in the gardens leading down to the river. Walter Greaves's famous painting in the Tate, Hammersmith Bridge on Boat Race Day, comes alive.

It seemed an appropriate time to reminisce with John Herbert, son of Sir Alan Herbert, who still lives in the Georgian house by the Thames in Hammersmith Terrace, next door to the house where he was born and which was made famous by APH.

It is said that Sir Alan was once standing in his garden, watching the river as usual, when a pleasure-boat came chugging by with its cargo of sightseers. The man with the megaphone directed the trippers' attention to the north bank and boomed out, 'On the right you can see the house of A. P. Herbert, the late humourist.' APH looked on, amused.

The weatherbeaten face of Sir Alan Herbert must have been the most familiar on the Thames. He was a master of many trades – lawyer, MP, reformer of laws, ordinary seaman, soldier, novelist, writer of verses and parodies, musicals and Punch pieces; but he was finally probably best known as a great man of the Thames.

He taught himself navigation, enrolled in the Thames River Emergency Service, was at his river post when the last war was declared and, having lived on its banks for half a century was appointed a Conservator of the Thames. It has been suggested with good reason that his stretch of the river should be known as Herbert's Reach.

The four Herbert children, of whom John, now fifty-one and a director of Christie's, was youngest, all grew up with a natural love of the river. They all learned to swim and to sail at the bottom of their garden, and every summer they would stand in the mud at low tide and paint APH's converted canal barge with hearts and roses, all the Romany symbols of canal mythology.

'I suppose it was rather like people being brought up on a farm and taking to farm life like ducks to water,' says John Herbert. 'We took to the river like ducks. It's never occurred to me to want to live anywhere else.'

His earliest memory is of the high tide of 1928, when the river flooded all the gardens in the terrace. 'Our basement was our dining-room, and I remember being brought down there by my nannie to see the sludge, and the four-inch-deep mud, and the grandfather clock lying on its side. My father was rowing about the garden in a dinghy.'

Again in 1953 the tide rose to within inches of the garden wall: now glass barriers have been added all along the terrace gardens, with the additional advantage of saving one's champagne glass from being carried off in the breeze.

The river view has changed dramatically since John Herbert's childhood. 'There were always three lines of boats off the Terrace. Converted barges and old steam-picket boats, and all the houses down here had at least two or three dinghies.

'With the war they all had to go for security purposes, and they never came back. As you can see, all along the river bank it looks sadly rather naked.' It does, especially at low tide. Nothing sailed by for an hour at a time.

'In the thirties the whole of the Port of London was so much busier. From Tower Bridge all the way down to Greenwich is now just a toothless mouth, with gaps where the warehouses have been pulled down. In the twenties and thirties you could see the bargemen bringing the barges up with just two great oars, and there were always processions of tugs and barges. Now, with containers, this trade has gone.

'In the thirties, too, the river was much cleaner, and there were great bathing parties. I remember looking out of my bedroom window, that little top window there, and watching Charles Laughton and people like that leaping into the river. Nowadays of course, except when we capsize, we don't leap into the river at all. And if we do we keep our mouths tight shut.

'There were plenty of fish in those days. I used to catch dace all the time and one of my sisters once caught a trout.

'It was an absolutely marvellous life. We would go down the river and get ashore at the Prospect, where the river used to be so exciting and is now sadly, virtually dead. The Prospect of Whitby used to be a wonderful place with a cranky old piano – not smart at all, up until the war.'

Hammersmith Terrace: 'the river is a special community'

John Herbert still has a fourteen foot dinghy, and sails at week-ends. But in the old days there were great family excursions in APH's famous *Water Gipsy*, three week trips and week-end parties, covering the Thames from the mouth to Oxford, and round into the Medway and the Crouch as well.

Lady Herbert was, fortunately, a keen sailor too, and the three daughters inherited the family passion; Jocelyn, the stage designer; Crystal, who lives by the canal at Islington and started a water-playground for children;

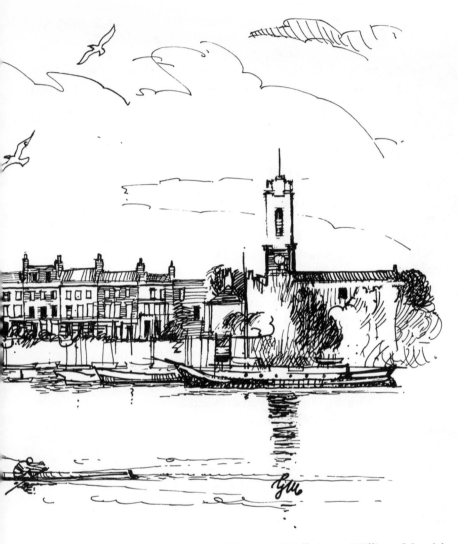

and Lavender, who lives along Chiswick Mall (near William Morris's Kelmscott House) and is heavily involved with Inland Waterways.

As he was being photographed, John Herbert was very conscious of how often Lady Herbert – observing from a window – must have watched his father being photographed in exactly the same situation, sitting on the garden wall looking down the river.

And the family album is dominated by river scenes: the devastation of 1928, the historic waterfront pub The Dove (James Thomson, who wrote

Rule Britannia, lived here, and it is owned and preserved by the local Chiswick brewers, Fuller Smith Turner), the boatyard where *Water Gipsy* was built, the smithies at Hammersmith hithe which gave Hammersmith its name.

Just beyond Hammersmith Terrace is Eyot Island, where swans until recently still nested, and where in the eighteenth century they made fishing baskets with the willow trees.

'I used to get up early in the morning, as a child, and drift up to the island, hiding beneath the gunwale, and see herons and swans nesting. There were swans in profusion, and tiny baby ducks. But as an island it's slipping. It is awash at high tide, and the herons don't want to come any more.'

How did these sixteen Georgian houses come to be built perilously close to the river's edge, and for whom, when behind them were open fields? 'I believe they were built as week-end homes for the prosperous middle class; various artists have made their homes here,' says John Herbert. Hogarth lived not far away.

Especially on Boat Race week-end, Hammersmith Terrace remains a village-like community. On the Saturday afternoon almost all the gardens, naturally, contained convivial parties, glasses clinking under trees and waiters serving buffet lunches; on Saturday evening Sir George and Lady Bull, at No 3, held a party for all those who had given parties.

'All of us here love the river. We're so lucky to live in Hammersmith: it is a village and always has been. All the way along the river is a special community. We got to know all the tug-masters and they always knew our family boat. Once they come here, people don't want to leave.'

Lady Herbert, who is an artist, painted the inn-signs for the two pubs in the neighbourhood, the now revamped Black Lion and the Old Ship. A walk along to the Black Lion, APH's old pub, was obligatory, even though its Skittle Alley is no more. Sir Alan was President of the Black Lion Skittles Club. 'It was a marvellous game,' says John Herbert. 'You threw an elliptical "cheese" at the ninepins at full pitch, and it was highly skilful.

'The landlord was a champion, and he gave marvellous parties for all the locals, with sandwiches and pickled onions, so there was a great community feeling.'

We looked for the skittle alley and found it was now a shed used for storing beercrates, but the sign remains: 'Silence on the throw please.'

Beyond the Black Lion, in Upper Mall, there used to be a waterworks and a chemical factory. Now there are walkways and concrete squares with benches, patches of green and Georgianized town-houses. 'This walk by the river is now opened up to hundreds more people to enjoy looking at what boats there are,' says John Herbert. 'It may look a little antiseptic but I think it's been done quite well. You can still look up and down the river and feel you are miles away.

'After a lifetime here people can't help feeling proprietorial and regretting certain changes. But change is inevitable. I remember when the Great West Road was built – it was essential, it had to come, but there was great debate in the thirties over the need for it, everyone getting terribly hot under the collar.'

While he was still an undergraduate at Oxford he wrote a book about the Thames, called *The Port of London*. He is rather bashful about it now. 'I was very naïve. It was for the Britain in Pictures series, and the absurd thing was that every other author was terribly well known, like Kenneth Clark. Oh, it was an awful book.'

'It wasn't that bad,' vouchsafed his son Robin loyally. Robin was at the time working on a trestle table in the garden, cutting a red sail for his model boat out of a pair of old pyjama bottoms. He was going to call the boat *Flying Eyebrows* ('like Vic Feather; he's got flying eyebrows,' he explained) and he insisted that his mother should paint the name in Russian, with a hammer and sickle. Mrs Gill Herbert, daughter of General Sir Brian Horrocks, was holding out.

Though John Herbert regrets that economically London is no longer the world's greatest port, he sees some advantages. 'The Thames is getting to be marginally cleaner again now. The wild life may return.

'In winter if you go along the far towpath, in the long grass at Chiswick Reach you occasionally put up a pheasant. And the other day I was burning driftwood on Eyot Island – great baulks of timber, like sleepers, frightfully dangerous because it could rip your centreboard and rudder off – and I almost trod on a snipe.'

CHAPTER EIGHTEEN

Elizabeth Longford
Harley Street

I had a mental picture of Lady Longford's childhood: an Edwardian nursery life, a large family, liberal and cultured, privileged and secure, disciplined but happy. It is the kind of childhood atmosphere she provided later for her own eight children.

Elizabeth Longford was the eldest child of two doctors, born at 108 Harley Street in 1906. In those days an ophthalmologist like her father, N. B. Harman, would live above his consulting rooms. Even today, when medicine has pushed most residents from this dignified Georgian street, Lady Longford's brother John still lives and practises in the house where he was born.

So it was no trouble to look inside the house, changed only by the addition of a lift for patients. Her parents' portraits still hang in the waiting-room. We could creep up the stairs just as she did in childhood: 'We were forbidden to talk from that stair to *that* stair. If we even whispered, a furious figure in black pinstripe would bounce out of the consulting room and shout "BE QUIET! How many times have I told you?" '

When her parents met, her mother, Katherine Chamberlain, niece of Joseph Chamberlain the Victorian statesman, had just qualified at the Royal Free Hospital. 'She had pulled out one tooth, and was paid £3 – I hope it was an impacted wisdom tooth for that – and she never practised again. She married instead.'

Father was born in Muswell Hill, seventh of twelve children but the first to survive infancy. The others had been carried off by diseases such as measles. 'I can still remember the little house in Muswell Hill, and my grandmother in what I see as black bombazine, exactly like Queen Victoria.

'They were a prosperous lower middle-class family, definitely a much lower social bracket than my mother's family, who had broughams. That's broughams, not brooms! They had housemaids to handle those.

'Christmas at the Chamberlains in Birmingham was a tremendous blow-out, with sucking pig. I was taken more than once to see old Joe Chamberlain, and I remember him in a wheelchair in his great mansion, across the way from my grandparents.

'Well, father went ahead very splendidly with his eyes, and got this house in Harley Street where we were all born.'

Elizabeth Longford was particularly delighted to be given, after the publication of her Wellington biography, a letter written by the Iron Duke in his barely legible hand, to his house agent in London: 'It appears to me that the house you mention in Harley Street opposite No 11 is very dear. I shall therefore be satisfied with No 11 unless you should hear of one that would suit me better at a reasonable expense.'

Life for the five Harman children hardly extended beyond Harley Street and Regent's Park, and was centred, of course, on their nurse. 'A tremendous Cockney character called Robbins. She was a wonderful comic actress who did all the things that nurses are not supposed to do. She never kept her promises, she favoured the younger ones and made clear her preferences. All the faults that Spock said were fatal.

'Smacking was just nothing, she laid on the whacks. Once she banged me on the head with a saucepan and it came up in an enormous lump. I said I would tell mother and so she bribed me – my brother was so shocked that I should succumb to a bribe – with some *papier poudré* that ladies used to keep in their handbags. I was easily bought.

'But she did make life fascinating. She taught me the splits, her small rotund figure with the bright red curly hair, leaping into the air and landing flump on the nursery linoleum.

'And she made us do not strictly necessary things like drinking the skin on top of hot milk: even today if I see a piece of skin the size of a fingernail I have to throw the whole thing away. But she could also devise the most imaginative treats: one of her games was the Toys Coming Out to Play. She would arrange the toys so that when we came back from the Park the great question was, had the toys been out to play while we were out?

'And there would always be one toy, a naughty boy doll, apparently left behind in the scramble to get back into the toy cupboard before our return. I distinctly remember seeing his leg sticking out of the cupboard, and being convinced I could see it moving.'

Every day, 'unless it was black fog or pouring with rain', they went to the Royal Botanical Gardens in Regent's Park, now Queen Mary's Rose Garden. Then, it was private and you had to pay an annual fee. So the baby

Queen Mary's Gardens, Regent's Park:
'all the lucky nannies and children had constant amusements'

of the family was always made a Fellow, and could take the other children as guests.

'You didn't meet the masses at all,' said the future Labour candidate for Cheltenham. 'All the children were from Park Square, Harley Street and Wimpole Street. It was the most glamorous and exclusive part of my life.

'We were a great cortège of nannie, under-nurse, baby in pram, toddler in mail cart, and brother and me walking each side of the pram, holding on to the spring, up Harley Street, across Marylebone Road, into the Inner Circle. There, the nannies unpacked picnics and we played in whichever belt our nurse had adopted.

'The point about the Botanical Gardens was that all the lucky children and nannies who went there had constant amusements. There was the Alexandra Rose Show, where I saw Queen Alexandra driving in an open carriage, and I heard my nurse say her face was *enamelled*. "But how could she smile?" I said. "How could she eat?" and nurse refused to answer my silly questions.

'There was a platform half-way along the Broadwalk decorated with masses and masses of Alexandra roses, and on it a beautiful little girl with golden curls, with whom I fell completely in love, she was such a dazzling vision. And I've always had it fixed in my mind that the little girl was Barbara Cartland. I suppose it *might* have been.'

100

In and out of the Park, all the companions were neighbouring doctors' children: Myrtle next door, daughter of Dr Murray, whose nannie was subject to strange fits and turns; the children of Dr Cyriax of St Thomas's the daughters of Lord Horder, King George V's physician; and Peter and David (now Lord) Eccles, whose father was also a Harley Street doctor.

Church loomed large. 'Mother was a Unitarian, even more extreme Nonconformist than father, who had been intended for the Baptist ministry by his family. He became a Unitarian to be like mother. I had, of course, to wait for my father's death before I could convert to Catholicism.'

The Harmans abandoned their local Congregational church – the King's Weighhouse in Duke Street – when the minister introduced Romish practices, and would go all the way to Notting Hill Gate to worship on Sundays, walking back through Hyde Park. 'Sunday afternoon in Harley Street was wonderful. Very quiet. About tea-time the muffin man used to come and after tea we always played. And for our Sunday money, a penny or tuppence, we had to recite from Palgrave's *Golden Treasury*.

'Sunday was the only time in the whole week that my father unbent. Our Sunday lunch was called dinner, and it was held in the dining-room, at the huge mahogany table. Each week, after the first two courses and before dessert, the white tablecloth would be removed and the baby would be brought down from the nursery.

'And father would put the baby in the centre of the table, wrap it in the cloth, and shoot it up and down the table, amid shrieks of laughter.' A stern Unitarian's sense of fun.

Elizabeth was first sent to a Unitarian school in Frognal, Hampstead, but loathed it and stayed only one term. 'It seemed like every day going to a different country. I must have been a rather precocious and uppish little girl who always learned more verses of Macaulay or whatever; I'm sure I was intolerable.'

So though normally acquiescent rather than rebellious, she stamped her little foot and went to the school of her choice – Francis Holland in Baker Street: 'After being taught to read very efficiently by my mother, the greatest event in my young life was going to that wonderful day school.'

She also attended Mrs Wordsworth's Dancing School, near Baker Street, and thinks that perhaps her husband's sisters might have gone there, too. Lord Longford was brought up at exactly the same time in Bryanston Square: 'We probably walked past his grand house on the way from church.'

Though the impression of nursery life is strongest – Lady Longford is graphic in describing the scene with the nurses and babies, rocking horses and dolls' houses, herself sitting obliviously painting at a table under the

101

window, hoping to be Michelangelo – mother was not entirely left out of the business of bringing up the children.

'She was busy with patients much of the time, but I would shop with her in Marylebone High Street, which I would enjoy except for one horror. Once a month it seemed to me, we would go to Mrs Hunt's Registry Office to engage a new maid or cook. As we sat there interviewing candidates through a sort of grille it seemed to me that we were on trial for our lives.'

And mother was devoted to reading the classics aloud to the children, every day of their lives. 'It was something I carried on myself, with my own children,' says Lady Longford. Mother insisted that there were to be no whimsical name shortenings – 'it was Mother, Father and Nurse; it was made clear that shortenings were frivolous and a bad idea' – except that poor Elizabeth remained Betty until she went to Oxford.

'What we most liked about the Harley Street house then was an exciting room in the basement called the Dirty Room. A canary had once died and its body had been put in there, and it was rumoured that there were dead cats in among all the rubble and lumber. It became our Chamber of Horrors, kept locked, with a faint aroma of soot if you peered inside.'

With Oxford Street so near, it naturally became an extension of their playground. 'At about ten or eleven one of our favourite games was going into a crowded Oxford Street and scuttling between the shoppers and the windows, saying Excuse me, excuse me. It was a ridiculous game, purely in order to annoy.

'We were taken to Selfridges for Father Christmas. My mother thought it silly. And when we brought home our gifts she always said, "There, you see, there was nothing worth having." She was a sympathetic and kind woman, but so sensible, you see. We had to have our mad Cockney, to introduce the other element.'

CHAPTER NINETEEN

Dorothy Scannell
Poplar

Everybody in Poplar just after the turn of the century knew the Cheggies. It must have been hard to miss them, the boisterous Chegwidden family: mother, father and ten children, five boys and five girls. 'People take to our family,' Mrs Chegwidden always used to say.

Dorothy Scannell says it was because of her mother's magical, bubbly personality that the Cheggies never felt deprived. On the contrary they had a wonderful time of it, always getting into scrapes and adventures. Every Cheggie child would run home, never walk, and mother would be there.

They had enormously varied characters, the ten of them, from Amy with her Sarah Bernhardt manner and Arthur the elegant dandy, to Agnes the infant prodigy and Charlie the unruly sailor lad. Mother always stressed to them how lucky they all were, and how good God had been to them, for they had all their faculties.

Dorothy claims to have wished, as a child, to be the only child of rich parents; but she can't have known then how dismal and truly deprived that state would have been by comparison. And how dull. For everywhere she and I walked in Poplar's noisy, dirty streets, some extraordinary incident from childhood was recalled.

As we passed Poplar Hospital she recalled that her father had been there with pneumonia: the doctor who came to diagnose the disease actually ran from the house. Another time Dorothy had to take her sister Marjorie there, after she'd sliced her hand with a cut-throat razor. 'Oh look, Dolly, you can see my bones,' Marjorie said, continuing to chatter brightly all the way along East India Dock Road in the bus.

There was the time when brother Cecil rummaged in father's tool chest and discovered a live bullet which he poked unwittingly into the fire: it

Poplar Recreation Ground: scrapes and adventures

exploded across the room, went straight through sister Winifred's skirt and embedded itself in the dresser.

There was the day father was felled by a right upper cut from a daughter he was teaching to box, sinking to the floor with a dish of hot prunes dripping on to his bald head. Later the same day he was felled again by Dorothy dreamily removing his chair from beneath him: he was safer staying at work, he remarked coldly.

When father decided to keep chickens, he managed to raise only one out of the thirteen he'd bought: and the day the one surviving chick peered through the wire-netting, the cat next door came along and bit off its head.

Dorothy was walking in a daydream home from the public library another day, when her back was grazed by a plummeting body: a woman had made a suicide leap from a window above her.

One humdrum week-end, after a frightful thunderstorm in which hundreds of sparrows were found drowned underneath the oak-tree in the church gardens, a herd of elephants escaped from a local circus and demolished a fruit stall in the East India Dock Road. 'That's where the elephant came and ate up all the fruit,' Dorothy pointed out to me calmly as we walked along the high street.

And a few yards farther along: 'That's where my best friend Grace was run over and killed by a lorry.' Life in Poplar was, as Lady Bracknell would have observed, crowded with incident.

But for all the mishaps and the poverty, the regular visits to the Pledge Office to pawn father's suit, and the eking out of his plumber's wage of thirty shillings a week, it's the happiness and the laughter of her childhood

that permeates all Dorothy's memories. She even adored her school, Wool-
more Street, though she knew she was not supposed to like it, and all her
friends said Dolly Chegwidden was crackers.

No 3 Grove Villas was a classy address for their home in the heart of the
East End slums. Today it is still called Grove Villas, E14, but instead of a
row of two-up, two-down semi-detached cottages there is simply a brick
wall, part of the extension to Poplar Baths. Over the opposite high wall is
the Poplar railway line. Even her unsinkably cheerful mother confided
years later to Dorothy that when she first saw that house she felt heart-
broken.

But they were grateful for any sort of home. Father Walter Chegwidden
from Cornwall, was desperate for work; mother, a pretty country girl from
Wiltshire called Leah, who had been in domestic service, now had four
small children: they thought they were destined for the workhouse.

Fate intervened in the shape of Poplar borough council, who needed a
plumber: so father brought the family to Grove Villas, putting sulphur
candles in all four rooms to get rid of the bugs. Later, they moved to a
bigger six-room house down the road, No 13, too pleased to worry about
the unlucky number. They planted a lawn and a garden, the first in the
Grove.

The whole area has now been redeveloped with not unattractive low-
rise council houses, and a square and a play-yard with a pile of rubble and
walls crammed with slogans. About a dozen trees remain, in a rigidly
straight line: there used to be one in each front garden.

In Dolly's childhood it was a busy short cut through from the main road
to the docks, swarming with merchants and drunken seamen, lascars and
workmen. Today, as we stood there, not a soul walked by. Wasn't it quiet,
said Dolly.

On the corner of the main road is the headquarters of the Poplar Labour
Party, with paintings of early luminaries George Lansbury, Chas Key,
Dave Adams, Bill Guy, Sam March. 'My mother,' recalled Dolly, 'was the
only Tory in Poplar.'

And next door are the Poplar Baths, with the Victorian statue outside of
local merchant and benefactor Richard Green. Here Dorothy would go for
her Friday night bath. Sometimes she would wait hours, because Friday
night was dancing night and also pre-wedding night for local brides, and
there would be a queue of girls wanting baths.

Her baths were in the original building, built 1851 and demolished 1931.
The present Odeon-like building, which is also the East India Hall for
boxing matches, was erected in 1932, and 'contributed materially to the
relief of unemployment in the district', as the plaque above the swimming

pool records. Here you can still get a bath, too, for 15p, plus 1½p for soap, and 5p for anti-rheumatic compound.

Our next port of call was the Poplar Recreation Ground, which has hardly altered: tennis courts, putting, netball, roundabouts and swings. It was the scene of a nasty incident in Dorothy's childhood, when she was molested by a young soldier, who was caught and convicted.

Here too, is the white statue of an angel commemorating those five-year-old children who died on the day in 1917 when a bomb hit nearby Upper North Street Infants School. To Dolly, six years old at the time, standing in the Grove eating soft fruit from a bag, it was simply a scene of commotion with people running to and fro carrying children covered in blood. Eighteen children were killed and many injured that day. Much later Dorothy discovered that the local boy she married had been in school that day, and her brother-in-law still bears the scar on his head.

We took a look down Chrisp Street, the thoroughfare stretching from Poplar to Bromley-by-Bow, which for young Dolly was a real Casbah, a thriving market street.

Today, only a lone Burton's remains in that long street. Most of the other shops are boarded up or demolished. Because alongside the street, opposite the baths, is a modern shopping precinct, complete with a tower block, spruce shop fronts and deserted elevated walkways where pedestrians never bustle.

The bank is still on the corner of Chrisp Street – Dolly used to be uncommonly proud that her sister knew the bank manager's daughters, who lived above the bank. 'We thought of them like royalty.'

How different from Dorothy's memories it is, memories of noise and smells and music and life. 'Outside the pub people would stand drinking beer and spitting eel bones on to the pavement,' she says. 'There was a Jewish sweet-seller who had all the patter, as good as a music-hall turn, and a quack in a frock-coat and top-hat who sold patent remedies for intimate ailments. There was a gipsy in ear-rings selling love birds, and a huge credit draper's called Neave's, all hung with hob-nailed boots.

'And the blind bootlace seller and the flower lady with the huge breasts, and the wild rabbit woman, and Sukey's herb-stall, and a very grand emporium called Oxenham's, where we used to buy hair-ribbons for special occasions.

'I always had a pink ribbon, which I hated because I had reddish hair. My mother would always say it's not pink, it's crushed strawberry. It was all the same to me – I'd never had a strawberry.'

For an imaginative child, anywhere in the world becomes romantic, and Dolly was intensely proud of Poplar, despite its slum reputation. She appreciated the graceful spire of All Saints Church behind the high brick walls. She was proud that John Seager's bookshop employed girls who had been to university: established 1868, it's still there and bears the sign: 'Ships' Libraries Supplied and Maintained'.

Limehouse was her favourite place, grey and dreamlike. And to her the Blackwall Tunnel Gardens were the Bois de Boulogne, where the band would play and on Sunday evenings all the young folk would promenade to and fro. 'It was like living at the seaside,' she says, and it's true that gulls wheel in the air above us all the time. Now the Gardens are overgrown, and adjoin the roaring motorway into the Tunnel.

Dorothy insisted on taking a long trek to find the jetty at Blackwall Stairs that she remembered sitting on for hours, as a child. 'I feel as if I were six years old again,' she said 'watching my brother Len, who'd be about twelve, diving naked into the river.

'Another member of the family would get on a bus and take Len's clothes to Greenwich to wait for his arrival across the river, and the rest of us would frolic about in the bow-waves from the passing boats.' The manager from the oil refinery next door commented to Dorothy that even an adult swimmer would think twice about swimming in such a current and with passing vessels: the entrance has now been walled up for safety. 'Yes, I think the Cheggies must surely have had a guardian angel,' said Dolly Chegwidden.

CHAPTER TWENTY

Mary Stocks
Kensington

Mary Stocks' earliest memory is of being carried to the end of her road, perched on the shoulder of her father, a tall man wearing the Victorian doctor's livery of top-hat and frock-coat, into Queen's Gate on the day Queen Victoria opened the Imperial Institute.

The year was 1893 and Mary Danvers Brinton was then two. 'And cursed be those,' she says, 'who demolished the Institute seventy years later to make room for the banausic sprawl of the Imperial College of Science and Technology.'

Banausic is one of Lady Stocks' favourite words for the ugly, philistine, illiberal buildings that have replaced former glories of the Kensington she grew up in, and which as vice-chairman of the Kensington Society she battles valiantly to preserve.

Her Kensington was the epitome of comfort and security of middle-class life at the turn of the century. 'I was conscious of no fear of anything,' she says. 'Life was orderly, comfortable and supremely secure.'

We took a tour round her Kensington: from Millais' house onwards, at the approach of Gloucester Road, it manages to remain much the same as it was in her more opulent time.

And the house where she was born looks much the same, from the outside at least. It is No 8 Queen's Gate Terrace, rather less kempt than its neighbours, and when we went to visit it we found on the door a notice: 'Maison de l'Institut Francais'.

Sadly, to the lasting detriment of Anglo-French relations, Baroness Stocks was refused admittance.

So she reminisced from the street outside. 'This house belonged to my grandfather, and my parents went into it when they married. Life here was cushioned by domestic service.

'The nurse lived with us children on the nursery floor. The other servants slept in the attic, and you could hear the cook and parlourmaid tramping up to bed in the evening. The rest of their time they spent in the area.'
The area was the basement, stretching out under the gardens at the back,
with skylights, known as leads.

Behind the house, in her childhood, were the stables.

'My father was not a carriage owner; he hired a hansom every morning
at eight, which took him on his rounds to patients, and he was back at
eleven to see the few who came to him.'

He would supply them with the *Morning Post*, *Punch* and the *Navy List*
to read. He could not understand anybody failing to find the *Navy List*
enthralling, since he had wanted to enter the Navy but was made to follow
his father into medicine. In turn he dispatched Mary Stocks' younger
brother Ralph to become a Navy cadet at the age of twelve.

'My mother shopped at Barker, which was a very old firm,' says Lady
Stocks, referring to John Barker's. "I'm going up the High Street" was
the expression. She had an account there, and I still hear her saying, "Put
it down to my account. Brinton. B-R-I-N-T-O-N."

'On one occasion a wicked man heard her doing this, went in just after
her and ordered a very large York ham and a Stilton cheese and said, "Put
it down to Mrs Brinton's account and deliver it." Sure enough, at our area
door they were duly delivered, and our servants expressed surprise, and
the wicked man came along and said, "There's been a mistake; you seem to
have my order," and carried off the ham and the cheese.

'In the morning my mother used to go down and order the dinner and
interview the cook and see what was in the larder, and write down the
order for Barker.

'From this house I left to get married, at St Mary Abbot's, and then went
to spend our first night in the Grand Hotel overlooking Trafalgar Square.
It was the first night I'd ever spent in a hotel.

'That night we were taken to the theatre to see Miss Kingston, an old
family friend, play Great Catherine, and she made us a nice supper on a
chafing dish, and the next morning my brother came to see us off to Italy,
and brought us a lot of cakes left over from the wedding party at home.'

One of the totally unchanging elements in the neighbourhood is
Kensington Gardens. 'It was our playground,' she recalls. 'It seemed to
me enormous, illimitable. I can still recognize individual trees.

'There used to be a thing called The Well; you went down some steps
and there was a spring coming up with a sort of leaden cup on a chain. We
were not supposed to drink out of the cup. It was alleged by our nurse that
a number of children misused the place and rendered it unhygienic.'

109

Imperial College tower: saved

The big annual treat was a visit to the panto at the Coronet Theatre, Notting Hill Gate, now the Gate cinema. And then there were the museums: 'Do you remember,' a former nursemaid named Ethel wrote to Mary Stocks in 1954, 'how we used to roam around the museums, especially the Natural History? And I used to take you and Master Ralph to Lancaster Gate every Sunday morning when fine . . .'

This was the weekly visit to the grandparents, Sir Alexander and Lady Rendel, at No 44 Lancaster Gate. The Brintons were part of an enormous and accessible family circle around Kensington. And in Belgrave Square there was Great Aunt Emily.

She was the widow of that W. H. Smith celebrated in the *HMS Pinafore* song about the Ruler of the Queen's Navee. In his lifetime W. H. Smith refused the Viscountcy of Hambleden; Great Aunt Emily accepted it posthumously. 'This nowadays would have entitled her to a seat in the House of Lords,' says Lady Stocks. 'Luckily it didn't then, for though she was very handsome and ornamental, she was extremely stupid. And in old age more so.'

Mary's schooling was first at the Pestalozzi Classes in Clareville Grove, not far from home, and then briefly at Kensington High School. She points out her old arch-windowed formroom; the building is now part of Westminster Technical College. Later she went to the newly-opened St Paul's Girls' School, Hammersmith (prayerbook number eighty, she remembers) where she gave no indication of her later academic distinction – a First at LSE, teaching at Oxford, and becoming principal of Westfield College.

We go to gaze on the tower of the Imperial Institute, which the efforts of Sir George Thomson and Lady Stocks helped to preserve when the rest of the institute was demolished 'to make way for all this banausic muck' at the end of Queen's Gate Terrace.

'That white house on the corner,' points out Lady Stocks, 'was where Mr Baldwin lived when he came up from Worcester and established himself with Mrs Baldwin. Mother felt it incumbent upon her to go and call.'

Lady Stocks' memory is extraordinarily vivid, it seems to me. 'Oh yes,' she says, 'my memories of Kensington are unimpaired. Old people are like that, their memory rolls backwards. But I can spend a great deal of my time searching everywhere for my spectacles, and then find them on the end of my nose.'

All the three Brinton children have come home to Kensington in their advancing years: brother Ralph, now eighty, lives in Addison Avenue. The baby of the family, Joanna, 'who went to a boarding-school, and was very fashionable and extremely beautiful and always liked the society of the rich' lived in Paris for many years but has now settled in Duchess of Bedford Walk, off Campden Hill Road.

'I'm just beginning to get to know her,' says Lady Stocks.

We roam through the parts of Kensington dear to her, pausing for exasperated sighs at the hippiedom of the High Street. We stop in the preciously preserved Kensington Square, where Mrs Christiansen, secretary of the Kensington Society, lives in John Stuart Mill's house at No 18, next door to the house where Hubert Parry lived.

Lady Stocks tells a tale about a house at the far corner: 'That's where Thackeray entertained Charlotte Brontë when she became famous. She was very shy, and he got very bored, and went off to his club, leaving his wife to deal with the difficult guest.'

'There's been a bit of dirty work in Young Street,' remarks Lady Stocks, turning grim. 'They've started a nightclub, and the club patrons park their cars in the square and bang their doors and rev their engines on cold nights and make hell for poor Mrs Christiansen.'

111

Going back up Campden Hill Road we pass the site for Sir Basil Spence's new Town Hall. Lady Stocks has no doubt that it will be monstrous. What was wrong, she wants to know, with the perfectly good town hall they had already?

And so back to Aubrey Lodge, in the grounds of Aubrey House, where Lady Stocks lives – in a basement flat full of William Morris and de Morgan tiles, a heritage of the influence of her uncle Halsey Ricardo, the architect. She shares the flat with Susan, 'an Ordinary English White Cat'.

And she is happy to be in the garden of the house she knew as the Miss Alexanders' residence, a country mansion in the heart of Holland Park where there was in her childhood a great deal of tea-partying on Sunday afternoons.

'My only fear,' she says, 'is that the house and grounds may be taken over for Holland Park Comprehensive.'

The struggle to hold on to her Kensington goes on, and it has no more fiery fighter than Baroness Stocks. As she says in the preface to her new addendum to her autobiography, *Still more Commonplace*: 'With London, my relationship has been a simple one: the love of a child for its mother: deep and continuous; beginning with the dawn of consciousness and ending with death.' Baroness Stocks died in 1976.

CHAPTER TWENTY-ONE

Robert Barley
City

Robert Barley, like his father and grandfather before him, was a job-master. In the City of London they kept four hundred horses for commercial use, and their business lasted from 1850 right up till the Second World War, when it finally became certain that there was no longer any profit in the horse traffic business in the metropolis.

'We'd provide the hosses' – for Mr Barley pronounces it this way – 'for all the big City firms, who couldn't be bothered with their own stabling. They would hire from us under contract.

'My father supplied the London General Omnibus Company with twenty hosses a month. And he supplied Macnamara's, the mail people who held the Royal Mail contract for years before the State started running it. We provided horses for the Lord Mayor's Show every year, and for West End doctors who didn't keep their own carriages.

'Then we were very well known for our prison vanners. You wanted a unique hoss for a prison van. Plenty of weight about him, but he had to be able to trot on at twelve miles an hour. They only allowed so many minutes to carry the prisoners from Holloway or Pentonville or Brixton to the police courts, carrying twenty-two prisoners inside and a man with a gun at the back.'

Now, in his eighties, Mr Barley is still surrounded by hosses at the Knightsbridge Riding School which he owns. And though he doesn't get about easily, he was still driving carriages on special occasions (weddings, carnivals) a few years ago. His assistant, Miss Dixon, says: 'He could get a coach and four round all the little corners of the City where you couldn't manage a mini.'

Dressed far more like a City gent than a lifelong horseman, in bowler and pinstripe suit, Mr Barley rode with me back to the City in one of those offensive motor cars that took away his trade. But habits of a lifetime die hard: 'Whoa!' he would cry to the driver when he wanted to stop. 'Steady, now!'

His family's house was above the stables, in Cross Street, now South Place, between Moorgate and Finsbury Circus. It has now become just another City building, called City Gate House, headquarters of Louis Dreyfus and Co., the stockbrokers, plus dozens of chartered accountants, the odd tax inspector and the Sierra Leone Development Co.

Only the gateway remains from Mr Barley's old house. The whole street is City businesses, where there used to be a barber, a delicatessen, Ling's Hotel for commercial travellers, Probyn's the bottled beer people, a chemist, Winstone's the marble fireplace people, the Red Lion pub, and Dorling's the printers.

'Mr Dorling was clerk of the course at Epsom, and my father used to sell him a lot of hosses to draw the haymaking machines. A great man for having mares and foals about him. He'd pass our place every day on his way to the Epsom train, and stop to look round.

'Our yard stretched right back to the houses in Finsbury Square. We could stand 130-odd hosses there in stalls and boxes, and there was a big ramp that led upstairs where we stood another fifty odd.

'Out in the glassed-in yard stood the carriages. In one corner, called the Wash, three men were permanently employed doing the washing. Two night men cleaned the harness at night, and there was a big staff of horse keepers, one man to eight horses. We had unlimited coachmen. They got a guinea a week, and had to have a clean collar every day.

'When that gateway opened at five to six of a morning, there'd be a queue of eight or nine men outside hoping for a day's work if someone hadn't turned up. And if a man didn't show up till ten past six, he was out for the day – somebody else would get his job.

'We used to do a fair bit of business with Stock Exchange people. The stockbrokers might see one of our hosses at work, day after day, and in-quire about him. You see a seasoned horse is always more valuable, and they would want a horse they could send down to their house in the country for the wife to drive in a carriage.

'And there's no better education for a horse than to drive round the streets of the City. Standing outside shops, they know how to wait; in traffic all day long, they had to be docile.'

His father would go every year to the Lincoln Fair in April and buy thirty horses, which all had to be broken in the City. 'We broke all our young horses into harness after six o'clock in the evening in Finsbury Square and the streets round there. Many's the time I've had a young hoss

City Gate House: 'There's no better education for a horse than to drive round the streets of the City'

buck and kick right into that wall at the end of this street.

'In the early days we kept two permanent breakmen, just to drive and make young hosses. It was one of our breakmen, Harry Cord, who taught me to drive a team. And team driving has always been one of my greatest loves.'

One of the big events of their year was Goodwood week. 'We used to run two coaches each with four horses, to do the long drive down to Bognor and back, staying overnight at Horsham on the way.

'You had to have four extremely fit horses to each coach, to last the nine days' driving.

'The last year my father did that was in 1913. After the First World War he never did it again. People were different-minded after the war. Who wanted to ride in a coach for two days at a stretch?

115

'Yet a coach is the only vehicle you can see the countryside from properly. The whole charm of driving was being up there on top. I remember in 1937 driving a carriage up to Edinburgh and toured Scotland with a party, and the view of the highlands you got from up there was marvellous, unbelievable. It's the only way.'

Looking along the grey façade of the City Gate House, Mr Barley recalled: 'They started pulling all this down and rebuilding it in about 1918. You'd be surprised what we had to put up with, still living here. They started demolishing that end, and left us standing in the middle till last. We stood there alone like an island till 1938. Then, of course, we had to go.'

Mr Barley's father lived to see the end of his commercial horse business: he died in 1942 at the age of ninety-two. And his eldest son had stayed with him in the business until the end – having joined him while he was still at school, helping at the age of ten.

'At fifteen I drove my first team to the Derby. I remember we took nine coaches there that day. I'd drive in the evenings after I'd finished at the Central Foundation School, Cowper Street, and I rode at week-ends in Hyde Park or a long ride out to Epping Forest. Mostly I drove; plenty of ponies and traps about then. And not a soul in the streets of the City on Sundays or after six in the evening.

'I loved it, being around the hosses. It was the only thing I was ever interested in in my whole life.'

In 1925 he married and moved out to Highbury New Park. But he still daily commuted to the City, by tram to Moorgate or, if it was very early in the morning, by pony and trap which called to pick him up. But by this time he could see that there wasn't much of a future in the business.

'The first thirty years of my life were my happy years. By the time I was a young man, after the First World War, I realized that the commercial hoss business was on the downward path. We were losing hold every day.

'In 1918 we still had four hundred commercial hosses at work. By 1920 we were down to less than a hundred. When all those motors flooded the market after the war, that was the death of the commercial hoss, and the red light for the whole harnessed trade.

'The proper thing to have done was to go into the motor trade. But my father didn't care for motors and neither did I. We weren't motor-minded. I still don't regret that we didn't do it. Other people did, and in the end we were the only job-masters left in the City. My brother Charlie went into the motor trade in '38.'

The years between the wars, the Barleys found themselves a new niche, supplying horses for the Territorial Army. In the First World War Robert junior had been scouring the country for horses to sell to the Army, supplying three hundred in the first fortnight of the war. In the twenties, during the Territorial year they would supply three to four thousand horses.

'In 1937 or 1938, I remember, the Army went on manoeuvres in the south of England to find out whether the Army would mechanize or not. We supplied the horses for Eastern Command – sixteen hundred horses for six weeks. Well, the Army decided to mechanize, didn't they?

'And the result was, we gave Hitler all our best horses. Well that's how it seemed. The Army sold off two hundred horses at a time at public auctions, and the majority were bought by foreign buyers. So Hitler had the pleasure of having all these fully-trained horses.' Mr Barley clearly thinks that mechanizing the Army was a bad idea.

Mr Barley had found himself a different style of life with horses. 'I took the Marble Arch riding school, though I still helped my father who was getting to be a very old man. I bought the school off a man named Charlie Cuthbert, when there were only eight horses; I increased it to twenty-one. And people weren't so horse-mad as they are today. But everybody who was anybody still rode in the Park every day.'

Later he had another riding school in Williams Mews, Kensington, and then in Queen's Gate Mews, and finally now he is in Elvaston Mews, with his fourteen beloved horses and ponies. He would have more if only he could expand his stabling premises. He has been providing horses for film work since the 1920s and one of his Palominos, called Golden Boy, was in the recent *Boris Godunov* at Covent Garden.

But it is easy to sense that he is happiest by far in the City. He still knows his City backwards, despite it being 'so altered I can hardly recognize it', and he deplores the traffic regulations and one-ways, harking back to the days when there was a policeman on point duty at every junction to direct the horses.

At the most unlikely places he will point out the sites of former stabling yards where they kept their extra horses: in Plough Yard, under the railway arches of Curtain Road, now all warehousing yards; in Pickard Street, City Road, now the site of a block of flats; and in Blue Yard, Duncan Street, Islington, now a National Car Park.

He looks for the Barbican Horse Repository, and the London General Omnibus Company's five-hundred-horse yard in Pitfield Street.

Outside Bart's Hospital he remembers visiting an injured man he had run over in his pony and trap in the Goswell Road. 'We asked him what made him run out under our pony, and he said, "It was either you or the motor car coming the other way. You were the lesser of two evils." The man survived. A car would have finished him off.'

117

CHAPTER TWENTY-TWO

Irene Handl
Maida Vale, St John's Wood

It seems apt that the delightful Irene Handl, whose stage-voice has the timbre of the shabby-genteel, should have been born in what was the perfectly shabby-genteel area of Maida Vale.

Her father, Frederic Handl, arrived in London in the 1890s from Vienna, with his French wife Marie. They had met in Brussels, and ran away to marry because all the parents disapproved of the match. 'He came over with absolutely nothing and went into a bank for about £90 a year. Then he worked his way up to the Stock Exchange, and finally he became a banker in a private bank in Throgmorton Street.'

The runaway pair ('they knew not a soul; they were orphans of the storm') found a home in a mansion flat in Maida Vale, there their second daughter Irene was born 'on a night of fogs, the end of a week of fogs so thick that link-boys were running about with candles and lanterns, lighting the way. A terrible pea-souper.

'The doctor was late, having lost his way – he almost went into the Serpentine. And the nurse was late too. Nobody could see where they were. The fogs in those days were the colour of that wallpaper; worse, a dreadful sulphurous green. I found them rather thrilling.' It was December 1900, shortly before Queen Victoria died: a convenient birthday, since she always knows she is as old as the century.

Irene Handl never married. She has lived most of her life companionably with her widower father until his death at eighty-seven, looking after the household. 'Housekeeping used to take far more time,' she says. 'You made all your own jams, and I still do, dear. I don't go in for packet stuff.'

The life must have prepared her well for the endless charlady roles that she does so superbly. But it concealed the sharp wit of the lady who has written, in longhand that ruined her eyesight, two bestsellers as well as immortal comedy sketches like the classic *Shadows on the Grass*, for herself and Peter Sellers.

On our trip to Maida Vale, we came to her old school, now called Paddington School, on Elgin Avenue. 'Oh!' she said. 'The almond's out' (a light dusting of pink blossom in the gardens of the mansion block opposite). 'I never thought I'd see an almond so early in the year.' When she and her sister attended the school, from kindergarten to leaving at fourteen, it was a fee-paying school run by a trust, Maida Vale Girls' High School.

'It was a very genteel place, a typically old-fashioned high-class girls' school, where monitors would run after you to see you'd got your gloves on as you left.'

Elgin Avenue has seen days both better and worse.

'These mansions flats were some of the first flats, and respectable people in those days didn't live in flats. A lot of them were occupied by what they used to call actresses but were really tarts, ladies who'd been what they called *installed*.

'But of course my parents weren't English and they didn't think about houses in the way they did over here.'

Their flat was behind Elgin Avenue, behind the late-Victorian and the 1920s mansion-flats with their wrought-iron balconies, a block called Leith Mansions in Grantully Road, directly overlooking Paddington Recreation Ground. The Handls lived at No 13, but she is amused to see that this is now called 12A. She thinks the block has run down: 'Boy!' she kept exclaiming at the peeling paint.

'I never liked this flat. I know I was only seven when we left, but I managed to dislike it before then.' She looks out at the view over the Rec, where there used to be music on the bandstand in summer, and sledging on tin trays in winter. 'I hated the Rec. A strange feeling comes over me when I see it, a peculiar feeling I've always had.'

The family's next move, to St John's Wood, was much more to her liking. 'We simply moved across the Vale, to the artistic quarter where all the artists lived, because of the art school in Circus Road.' They went to Melina Place, a quiet little back-water of mid-Victorian houses among the towering canyons of typical St Johns' Wood flats.

Here the Handls lived for fourteen years, at No 11 and at No 9. She notes that what has always been the prettiest of corners is now choked with parked cars: each house has now a garage, not to mention modish innovations like chintzy shutters, burglar alarm systems, twee lanterns and pastel washes. They look fine to me but Miss Handl is dismayed.

'The point about these houses was that they were charming and simple,

Melina Place: '. . . just very, very pretty. The hallmark of St John's Wood'

with big gardens and studios for artists.' Of all the houses No 9, she
thinks, looks most as it did before, with a fig-tree in the garden, and a
garret in the roof where Irene could have her friends in. Next door there
used to live an old lady with an electric landau – 'it was completely silent:
they should bring them back'.

No 11 is now pink, and called Pear Tree Cottage. It is owned by the
actress Yolande Donlan, who once showed Miss Handl photographs of
the way she converted it. 'She put in a swimming-pool, and our old coach-
house became an executive flat, and the wash-house became an office.

'I would hate,' added Miss Handl, 'to live anywhere that had been
improved beyond recognition.'

'I remember this road with such affection. We had two owls in our
garden, a squeaky one and a little hooty one. And a squirrel that collected
nuts. It was just very, very pretty. The hallmark of St John's Wood. None
of these blocks of flats there then, of course.'

From there the family had to go to Switzerland, because Mrs Handl had
to go to a clinic, where she died of cancer. They were an immensely close
family, and the bereavement seems to have affected Irene Handl deeply:
she says little of her late teens and twenties, only saying mysteriously: 'It's
like one of those black holes that the stars are supposed to have, dear.'

120

In the picture of herself in her teens she has a big bow in her hair and an expression of self-mockery in her laughing eyes.

'Yes, I was a pretty girl,' she agrees. 'I went to America for a holiday in the middle of the Prohibition era, and was proposed to by various people. There was a man who had a chain of hotels – I'd have been a multi-millionaire by now – and another man in pictures, which were going great guns then. And in Paris I was proposed to by a famous car manufacturer's son.'

And she turned them all down? 'Well, I was a very strange person. I just knew I wanted to . . . do my own thing, you'd call it now. I felt very acutely that I wanted to be free.'

In retrospect, she realizes that what should have happened to her was that she should have taken to the stage, and to writing, much earlier. 'But we didn't live in either a literary or a theatrical circle, and so I just burst into both worlds much later.' Her mother had been a talented amateur actress when they wrote and performed their own dramatics at home, so she supposes she must have inherited that.

What she did instead doesn't sound like freedom, but it was enjoyable: life with father in a succession of London flats: Northgate, Regent's Park; Devonshire Hill, Hampstead; Clifton Court, the mock-Tudor key flats on the corner of St John's Wood Road; Berkeley Square; Brown's Hotel; Dorset House, Baker Street; Bayswater Road – and now, since her father died, home is a sunlit mansion flat with vast bay windows in Chepstow Place, shared with her chihuahuas to whom she talks in incomprehensible Dog Language.

Until 1937, when she took to the stage and instantly captured the West End with her non-speaking début as an inept parlourmaid in *George and Margaret*, it was a life of housekeeping, shopping, social visits and the cinema, theatre and music-hall, with no financial worries. The favourite outing was on Fridays to the Met in Edgware Road, the famous music-hall.

And they went abroad every year, to relatives in Paris and Vienna. 'I'm very fond of abroad, you know. Directly the dogs die, I don't buy another for a year, and go abroad. When Foxy died [a Pom that bit people] I went for a year to Australia and New Zealand. I long to see the world.'

However, work binds her to London. 'I am a Londoner, and I never left, even during the Blitz. But I don't feel the same allegiance to her now. I'm sick of her. I am thoroughly out of love with her.

'London is only comforting if you're young. You'll wait hours for transport and nobody seems to be a Londoner any more. Cockneys used to be good-natured, like country people only sharper-witted. And the look of the place! Nobody lifts a broom. Oh, they do houses up with gallons of paint, but the hedges are untidy and the litter – I'm afraid it's going the way of New York.'

CHAPTER TWENTY-THREE

Jack Dash
Elephant & Castle

"Rockingham's just all right by me" are the cheerful words emblazoned across a corrugated iron barrier in Rockingham Street, near the Elephant and Castle. It is the barrier of an Adventure Playground.

When Jack Dash lived there Rockingham was all right by him too, but then it was terraced cottages with mews behind, and a cobbled street where kids had their own Adventure Playground on their doorstep.

He was, he says, a real street urchin: an orphan, without boots on his feet; but wildly happy because life was a ceaseless round of street games. When Jack Dash talks about them he is beaming and mellow and seems altogether a softer person than the erstwhile scourge of the dockyards.

Unlike most dockers he didn't come from a docking family. His mother was a music-hall actress, Rose Gertrude Johns, who outraged her family by marrying a stage-hand and scene-shifter, Thomas Dash. 'The Johns were petty bourgeois, middle class,' says Jack Dash, and, never one to miss the chance of a spot of polemic, adds: 'Of course, there is no middle class any more. They maybe think they're different but they're not. Everybody has to graft for a living.'

The Johns' disapproval was in some measure vindicated when their son-in-law lost his job and they were obliged to give him a job rent-collecting in a tenement they owned in Hoxton called the Haberdashers Estate, a pretty rough neighbourhood.

'Everything was fine for a while. But my Dad was a great entertainer, a good sport, and a great story-teller. He started letting people off their rent so they could throw parties which he would go to and provide the entertainment. When the Johns found out about that they sacked him. After that he couldn't get a job anywhere, and poor mother had to clean bar-rooms to feed us and keep a roof over our heads.

Rockingham Street Adventure Playground:
'We was weedy little kids, not like the children today'

'I was much too young to remember it, but my three older brothers told me she often walked the streets with me in her arms, singing to get a few coppers.

'They would come home to find mother sitting outside the house on an upturned bucket, crying, all the furniture taken away.

'Finally she was worn out by all the undernourishment and the long hours of scrubbing filthy floors. She died of consumption at the age of forty, when I was seven.'

One of their houses in those days was 1 Launcelot Street, just off Lower Marsh, SE1. It looks exceptionally pretty, festooned with geraniums and climbing plants.

'Now, did we do a moonlight flit from here, or were we evicted?' Jack ponders. 'I think it was a moonlight flit.'

All the noise and bustle of Lower Marsh street market is a few paces away, round the corner. The trader who was attracting most attention on that day was flogging a batch of flash gigolo-style sun-glasses, even though it was raining hard ('Tory weather, as we used to say in the docks,' said Jack).

'Every evening, about a quarter to nine, people would be waiting for the perishable food to be auctioned off: women in black shawls surrounding the butcher in his striped apron, holding up the meat under kerosene lamps. The stallholders called it being "at the murder", murdering their prices.

'And if us kids could find an overripe banana on the ground that was a luxury. Then we'd collect up any orange-boxes we could, and sell them for firewood, and share the proceeds. Poverty's easy to share, you see; it's riches that's difficult to share.'

Naturally, Jack is a demon user of rhyming slang. But in the markets you'd also hear Cockney back-slang. 'Well, if you was in a shop and asked the butcher how much for that bit of meat, he'd call the guvnor and it'd be: "What's the scrip?" "Neves". Sevenpence a pound. Then they could vary the price according to the look of the customer. Or if you wanted to make a remark about some girl without her hearing, you'd say: "Evah cool at that elrig's sgel!" Have a look at that girl's legs!'

After a brief time in various orphanages, Jack went to live with his father and two elder brothers in just one upstairs back room of the house his aunt and uncle had in Rockingham Street.

His old man, never in work, did what he could to get food: beg, borrow, and a bit of ingenious thieving. Like the night he was prop man at the old Elephant and Castle theatre, and came home on Saturday night bearing a beautiful white Angora rabbit.

It was one of the conjuror's rabbits that emerged from a top-hat and jumped over a wand; Dad made it jump over a broom-stick and into a large saucepan. It fed them for two days.

'I'll never forget the working-class mothers of Rockingham Street. Because I had no mother I was always welcome at their kitchen tables – and those kitchens, to me, were luxury, where the kettle and stove were so black-leaded you could see your face in them. They gave what they could, even though they had so little for themselves.

'Specially Mrs Boyce, who had fourteen kids but would still come out searching for me, shove a thick slice of bread and treacle into my hand and say: "There you are, son, get that down yer. I wish it could be more." That was always the line: "I wish it could be more." '

In those days all the terraced streets around the Elephant led up to the circus, with its Trocadero – the Troxy – and its shops. 'I've seen about a thousand people gathered in the circus outside Montagu Burton's, the fifty-bob tailor, watching those scintillating lights that give you the news because Burton had the bright idea of giving boxing commentaries round by round, whenever there was a big fight, say Kid Lewis. I remember standing there when Beckett got knocked out by Carpentier.

'But then, anything would bring people out into the street. Even to see an aeroplane was an event that brought us rushing out. The boys would shout: "Aeroplane, aeroplane!" and out we'd run. Or a balloon! "Baa baa balloon! Baa baa balloon!" was the cry.

'We had our street games for every season: you'd never play with whipping tops when it was the skipping-rope season. Or alley gobs with stones, when it was marbles all along every kerb.

'At Easter, Good Friday, there'd be communal skipping in the street, whole families joining in. They'd get a heavy rope, borrowed from the docks, and the fathers and eldest sons would turn the rope for the mothers and daughters.

'We were cheeky children of course – you'd poke your tongue out at an adult and run away – but there was far more deference for adults, too. You see the spire of Trinity Church? It has a statue of 'Arold, and if any of the mothers wanted to frighten us, they'd say the ghost of 'Arold would come and get us.

'You could walk into anybody's house, any time, the doors always open. This was a community. There was life in the street, outside. The cat's meat man would come by and put the meat on a skewer on the doorsteps, because everybody had a cat, for the rats.

'The hurdy-gurdy man would come by and you'd give him a couple of old jam-jars – there's always been money in salvage. Then the rag and bone man: "Old rags for china!" and for a few old rags you'd get cups and saucers. And the occasional Indian in a turban, selling Indian toffee.

'We earned pocket-money by doing errands. And when we got it, we would dive straight into the baker's for hot buns and rolls. Not sweets! It was bread we wanted, people like me. Dive straight in there, hot cross buns four a penny, a farvin' each!

'We was weedy little kids, nothing like the children today who really are adults physically. And in that cruel way that children have, everybody got a nickname. Cuffy, for the boy who always had a runny nose and wiped it on his sleeve; Bossco or Swivel-eye for anyone with a squint, Carrots or Ginger or Rusty for red-headed lads, Lofty or Lanky or Nipper or Titch or Shorty, Limpy or Gammy for the lame – and if your name was Smith you was always Smudger. Me, I was always called Jackie though. I suppose I asserted myself, even then. It must have been my theatrical family background.

'There was one of our lads called Charlie, who had a glass eye. Some days we'd all go off walking in a gang to Hyde Park – that was our countryside – and swim in the Serpentine. Then we'd get Charlie to do his act. He'd take out his glass eye, give it to one of us to look after, and then stand near the old dears in their deck-chairs and sob loudly.

'When they asked what was wrong, he'd tell them he'd lost his glass eye and his dad would wallop him. It never failed: They'd dip into their purses for a few coppers . . . pretty soon we'd have enough for a bus back to the

Elephant and a blow-out at the coffee shop: a pair of kippers, two thick slices and a big cup of tea. It was like Balshazzar's Feast to us.'

Today, nearing seventy he is still leading and organizing – he's a champion of the old-age pensioners now – Jack Dash lives in a tower block in Stepney. Naturally, he runs the tenants' association and naturally they have taken on the GLC over rents. 'What vestiges is left of community life, of village life, in London, is kept alive by the tenants' organizations,' he says.

'I am London,' he says. 'I helped to build London. When I was in the building trade, before I went into the docks, I helped to build roads, houses, cinemas, all over London. I worked on the Police College at Hendon. I helped to build the Royal Commonwealth Club near Trafalgar Square – never dreaming at the time that I'd one day be invited back to lecture!

'I learned my first beginnings of trade-unionism at the Astoria, Streatham. And come to think of it, I led my first strike at the Odeon, Mile End Road.'

CHAPTER TWENTY-FOUR

Sir Osbert Lancaster
Notting Hill

A dear little boy named Osbert, in a blue silk suit with Brussels lace collar and buckles on his shoes, is handing round petit-fours and cucumber sandwiches to ladies perched on Hepplewhite chairs, drinking tea from best china out of a silver teapot: the childhood of cartoonist Osbert Lancaster is straight out of Hilaire Belloc's *Cautionary Tales*. He would be one of the *good* little boys of course.

These rigidly formalized teas would take place every Thursday, which was Mrs Lancaster's At Home day, in Elgin Crescent, Notting Hill.

It was all part of the social pattern observed in Edwardian Bayswater and points west – a culture which has now vanished. It was, though it did not call itself by such a name, the upper middle-class way of life. And while the aristocracy is far from gone, and the lower-middles and middles are abundantly increased, 'the old upper-middles', Osbert Lancaster says, 'are as extinct as the speakers of Cornish'.

In search of these *temps perdus* we set off on a walk from the parish church of St John's, Notting Hill, in Lansdowne Crescent: a focus of family life for the Lancasters. Young Osbert once sat on the knee of Prebendary Webb-Peploe, whose evangelical sermons would regularly cause members of the congregation to be carried out on stretchers.

Lancaster senior was a churchwarden, and his death at the Battle of Arras in April 1917 is commemorated inside the church on a plaque.

The other churchwarden, says Osbert Lancaster, 'was a terrifying old boy with a squint. Sir Aston Webb, president of the Royal Academy, and architect of the west front of Buckingham Palace in the then current Potsdam style. Built himself an extraordinary house south of Ladbroke Square, a very advanced 1911 job.'

From the church we walked down Kensington Park Gardens. I can imagine few things more pleasant on a fine, blowy day in early spring than accompanying Mr Lancaster, with his bow-tie and cane, along this sumptuous road of towering palazzi, individual without being eccentric. 'The work of an architect called Allom,' says Lancaster. 'The best are really quite distinguished. The detail of the cornices and the pilasters is so scholarly.

'Just off here, on Stanley Crescent, I went to kindergarten at the house of an old boy named Baxter, who was mayor of Kensington. One of those early kindergartens where one made models of Hiawatha's tent, that sort of thing.'

Down Ladbroke Grove he pointed his cane. 'Those traffic lights *there* marked the end of respectability. Beyond there were fearful slums, where all the fences lived. Nannie would tell me that policemen had to walk in pairs there.'

On the corner of Lansdowne Crescent lived the stooping, walrus-moustached Colonel Hook: 'A marvellous old boy.' Lancaster remembers Colonel Hook's study as the most vivid interior of his childhood, and the most distanced from the twentieth century. With its faded sepia photographs of whiskered brother officers with topees and swords, it was redolent of stockades and last stands, fuzzy-wuzzies and Pathan knives. Now Colonel Hook's house is a block of modern flats.

In this area, some of the oddest graffiti in London are to be found. On the corner of Arundel Gardens, for instance, sprayed on the blank concrete, are two legends: 'There is no normal' and 'Beware the thundrous [*sic*] trowel surgeons.'

'The Ladbroke Estate was all so frightfully well planned,' commented Osbert Lancaster, putting on his hat as adviser to the GLC Historic Buildings Board. 'It's the high point of Victorian town planning. All these quiet streets, and the bliss is that they all back on to large communal gardens, where the children could be tossed out to play.

'Every one of these houses was lived in by a single family. Even though my parents, when I was born, must have had a joint income of no more than £600 a year, they maintained a cook, a nurse, a boot-boy and a house-maid – that was Kate, centre of my below-stairs world, who sang all the music-hall songs.'

And so to Elgin Crescent itself, the graceful curve of mid-Victorian semi-detached villas, each with three floors and basement, and pillared porticos and mouldings in the classical style of the neighbourhood. Originally, they were all creamy stucco, gleaming underneath the cloudless pre-First World War sky. Later, during the Second World War,

Kensington Park Gardens:
'The old upper-middles are as extinct as the speakers of Cornish'

Osbert Lancaster revisited the Crescent to find that it had completely gone to seed.

Having seen its worst days, Elgin Crescent is today resuscitated, reverted to its posh origins. 'Dear me, what a deal of prinking up there has been here,' said Lancaster, surveying the burnt oranges and persimmons, Wedgwood blues and primrose yellows and chocolate browns of the façades.

All was spruceness without and, through the sunlit windows, Habitat within. Scrubbed pine tables in the basements, Indian rugs and squashy sofas and William Morris curtains on the ground floors. 'After the war, you see, people came swooping back here – tele-producers and Roy Jenkins and the like. A new and comparatively well-heeled world has returned to the area.'

And then we came to No 79, the house formerly occupied by the extraordinary Madame Blavatsky, and in 1908 the scene of Osbert Lancaster's birth. We stared in disbelief.

No 79 was the only house on the Crescent which was derelict: the windows boarded up with corrugated iron, the stonework crumbling, balustrade broken, garden completely overgrown.

Round the back, among rotting cabbages and an old wrecked pram, we discovered that there were fresh daffodils in a vase in one window, so it must be occupied still by someone. 'How dreadful,' mused Osbert Lancaster, 'that the one blot on the street should be my birthplace.

'And how unfair that Mrs Ullathorne's next door should be so beautifully done up.' Mrs Ullathorne was a heavily-painted *grande dame*, who had enjoyed considerable success at the court of Napoleon III, and would bid the tiny Osbert to tea at intervals, and make him kiss her hand and bow.

The atmosphere of these quiet roads in mid-morning is distinctly unmetropolitan. Occasionally, you see someone walking a dog, or bicycling. Not much traffic about. The roads are generously endowed with trees; in his childhood, Lancaster recalls the air being, all summer long, heavy with the scent of limes.

'And on early Thursday evenings, the Italian organ-grinder would come by, and the children would be sent out in the street with pennies. In those days Italians looked like Italians, straight out of *Cavalleria Rusticana*. And there was an old gentleman who would come out on winter evenings to play the harp by the street-lamp in the fog.'

Since the most vital feature of his childhood was the daily walk to the Round Pond with nannie, we took the same journey. A perambulator, he thinks, is still the world's most pleasurable form of progression, rivalled only by the gondola.

On the corner of Ladbroke Square we passed his family doctor's house, a doctor who wore a frock-coat and a stethoscope tucked into his top-hat: 'very sensible place to keep it'. Opposite, where a huge block of flats stand, was the enormous house of Elmer Ambrose Sperry, the American who invented the gyrocompass.

We passed the point where the old balloon lady used to sit. 'She was so romanticized by James Barrie, who was an awful sentimentalist, and there was an Arthur Rackham drawing of her in her poke bonnet – but in reality she was horrible, *horrible*.'

The walk along Bayswater Road, up the Broad Walk via the Dutch Garden to the Round Pond had its daily excitements. 'Seeing a gull was an occasion. Nowadays, they're all down the Great West Road, but then it was the farthest place they reached up the Thames.'

CHAPTER TWENTY-FIVE

Muriel Box
Surbiton

Surbiton: the very name is synonymous with suburban respectability. Muriel Box, the film director and screen-writer who is now married to the former Lord Chancellor Lord Gardiner, remembers what it felt like to be a restless, ambitious teenager growing up in Surbiton: 'My paramount sensation was of being slowly stifled in a suburban brick-box from which there seemed small chance of escape.'

The brick-box is a solid three-storey Edwardian semi at 354 Ewell Road, a house now turned into three flats. It cost her parents about £1000 in 1906, Lady Gardiner remembers, far beyond their means, the payments always a struggle to find. 'Our family fell into the class known as the Respectable Poor. We were not only very conscious of our poverty, we were ashamed of it and always tried to hide it.'

The concealment was undertaken mainly by mother, Caroline Beatrice Baker, known as Bertie. She was a suffragette, a former schoolmistress, of volatile temperament and forthright and dogmatic views, who wore gold-rimmed spectacles and went to Fabian Society meetings.

It was she who found the house, which father, dapper Charlie Baker, a £10 a month clerk with the South-Western Railway Company, must pay for. To help out, he did a little bookmaking on the side, in the staff dining-room at Waterloo Station, where he went to work every day in silk topper and spats. His temper, too, was uncertain: and though he mocked the mugs who placed bets with him, his wife never forgot that he had himself gambled away the £100 they had prudently saved together before their marriage.

Later, she seized the purse strings; but before that, Lady Gardiner says, 'My earliest recollections are of daily bickering over money, which erupted into savage rows, and, on rare occasions, blows.'

When they weren't fighting about money there were plenty of other subjects to disagree over, like politics (Mr Baker was a Conservative) or music. Their piano duets ended always in waspish altercation, and Mr Baker was banished to the coal-cellar to practise his violin or smoke his pipe, both of which Bertie found intolerable.

At that time there were only half a dozen houses on their stretch of the Ewell Road: a manor-house across the road had stables behind, and beyond it stretched green fields with enormous dog daisies and buttercups. 'When I ran away from home at twenty, I didn't go back for ten years and when I did, oh! the shock I got. Brick-box building estates sprawled all over the Malden fields to meet the new Kingston By-Pass.'

Her infant life was distinctly rural. She would be pushed for miles in a go-cart by sister Vera or brother Vivian, along country lanes past farms and meadows, to eat picnic lunches of banana sandwiches beside a stream, and get milk from a roadside churn, and gather wild flowers.

Ewell Road is now a deafening thoroughfare. On Derby Day, Lady Gardiner remembers, since it was the main route to Epsom there would be a procession of every kind of vehicle from donkey carts to Rolls-Royces, and the Bakers would watch with amusement the changed expressions on the faces of the returning racegoers. It wasn't until she was sixteen that Muriel was taken by her gambler father to the Derby; in great glee they watched Captain Cuttle race home to win them £50.

Next door at The Briars there still lives Mr Colin Partner, who was born in the house and has never moved in sixty-nine years. His father, a business man who travelled often to America, was one of the victims of the *Titanic*. 'I remember seeing his mother in her bedroom, bowed over and weeping, every day for about six months. And I remember feeling, how terrible to be so broken by your husband's death. Within a week her hair turned white.'

In this respectable suburban house Muriel Baker lost her virginity (astoundingly early, at six) with the aid of a precocious playmate, and also her tonsils. The tonsillectomy was performed, as was the custom, at home.

'When I came round from the chloroform my sister showed me my tonsils in a bottle and I turned away thinking how horrible. When I was allowed up again, I asked to see them, but Vera told me I couldn't. "Why not?" I demanded. "Mother's given them to the cat," she replied. Nothing,' adds Lady Gardiner, 'was ever wasted in our house.'

Far more horrific was the accident which alarmed and dismayed the household and which Muriel witnessed at the age of six. Her eleven-year-old brother was standing on a stool by the stove, watching his elder sister cooking some fish. Startled by a spurting drop of fat, he knocked the

133

Derby Day on Ewell Road

handle of the pan full of boiling oil so that it covered him from head to foot. Lady Gardiner can show the doctor's house to which Vera fled for help.

Skin-grafts followed, at home and at St Thomas'; Vivian mercifully survived and at eighteen he passed as a crack shot into the Indian Army. He lives still in Ceylon. 'But for the rest of my mother's life she was haunted by what happened that day. She had been in bed with a poisoned thumb at the time, and deeply resented my father's blaming her for the accident.'

Lady Gardiner was sad to see, as she stood in the immaculate next-door garden, the deterioration of their own. 'What has become of the mass of rhododendron bushes? Where's the apple tree and the terrace and the climbing roses and the little path? The garden was my mother's pride and joy.

'All her life, my mother's hands were never idle for a moment. It hardly seems conceivable today, the time and trouble that simple housework involved. Just keeping the knives clean was a chore, polishing them after every meal or they'd go black. We were so thrilled with a wonderful new invention that was operated by a handle, for cleaning the knives with a pink powder; it made such a difference.

'Ironing was a great business of keeping two irons hot on the fire. The front doorstep had to be hearthstoned every week till it was snow-white – and surreptitiously, so that the neighbours couldn't see that we had no maid. The stove had to be laboriously black-leaded. On Saturday mornings we had to clean and polish every piece of brass, copper and silver. I still can't stand the smell of Brasso.'

134

Economy being essential, shopping was 'a misery'. 'Butter, tea, sugar and other groceries were immediately weighed by my mother on our return from the local shops, and if they were underweight we had to go back and demand redress.

'Sometimes we just couldn't afford to go to the local shops at all. Then my mother would pawn her wedding and engagement rings and on Saturday night one of us would go with her to Waterloo – since my father worked for the railway it only cost us about a penny – to shop in the Cut, the market just outside Waterloo Station. We would cram an enormous suitcase full of food for the week.'

Of course we had to go back to the Kingston Cinema, the first cinema Muriel Box ever visited – Sunday afternoon excursions to see cliffhanging serials, slapstick comedies and flickering newsreels. King Edward VII's funeral impressed her more than anything. The cinema is now called the Studio 7, opposite Kingston Station.

Round the corner in Fife Road, the old Super Cinema is now a Times Furnishing store. Muriel was privileged to sit with the projectionist here, since her mother knew the owner, Mr Cohen. One day she was told not to laugh so loudly: during Chaplin's *Shoulder Arms*, the audience was alarmed by the bursts of laughter coming from behind the screen.

The amenities of life do not alter too radically in places like Surbiton. The recreation ground opposite her home, where the tomboy Muriel joined a gang of boys in tree-climbing, is still there; the Assembly Rooms, grand Edwardian mausoleum, where light fantastics are still tripped; Surbiton High School where the white-haired Miss Proctor ruled like a martinet, stands also. Here is the Kingston Empire, where Muriel first saw variety shows and later had her own plays produced: and the Margaret Barnes School of Dancing, where the marvellous Miss Barnes (still alive, now in her nineties) demonstrated entrechats and pliés to the stage-struck Muriel before she was examined by Adeline Genée.

How Muriel broke away from Surbiton – and into films, becoming half of the thirty-year-long partnership of Muriel and Sydney Box – is told in her autobiography, *Odd Woman Out*. 'I used to think life was haphazard,' she told me. 'But while I was writing the book I found a pattern emerging. I didn't realize at the time how ambitious I was as a child, to do what I wanted to do really *well*.'

At fifteen she met by chance, on a train to Southsea, a film producer called Joseph Grossman. And once attracted to the idea of working in films and the theatre, Muriel Baker began to feel stifled by the Surbiton surroundings. Her first love affair there was prolonged and aimless: a man called Stanley who had a motorcycle and lived farther along Ewell Road.

He was a confirmed bachelor of thirty-three who, incapable of committing himself emotionally, finally married at forty-nine and died within a year. At the time he seemed to her the height of sophistication and taught her mathematics.

In the end, says Lady Gardiner, 'in need of breathing space in which to sort myself out away from everything and everyone, I ran away.'

She left the proverbial note on the dining-room table. 'Gone to the devil,' it crisply said. Actually, she confesses, she had gone to Dorking. With three shillings, a toothbrush, some apples and E. V. Lucas's *The Open Road* in her mac pocket: good-bye to Surbiton and hello to the big wide world.

CHAPTER TWENTY-SIX

Anthony Storr
Westminster Abbey

Certain corners of London seem to belong to the passing traffic of tourists, so it is easy to forget that people live there too. The precincts of Westminster Abbey, for instance: what is it like to be a child growing up with the overpowering Abbey just a few yards from the nursery window?

Dean's Yard was an extraordinary place to grow up in, according to the psychiatrist Dr Anthony Storr. When he was one year old, in 1921, his father became a Canon at Westminster Abbey, and the family moved into the official residence in Dean's Yard, just beyond the Abbey cloisters, a centuries-old house that once formed part of the monks' cellars.

He spent his first twenty years in that secluded and sheltered place. 'I was always conscious,' he says, 'of the feeling of privilege. The gates were locked at ten o'clock every night; one always felt protected and enclosed.'

Dean's Yard is a large, peaceful square with an expansive lawn and a spreading chestnut tree exactly opposite the front door of the Storrs' old home. 'I would look out of the window,' says Dr Storr, 'and if there was a Westminster School boy rolling the lawn, I would wonder what frightfully wicked thing he had done, because rolling the lawn was a Westminster School penance.'

By far the youngest child of his family, born unexpectedly late in his parents' lives, and with very few children of his own age around, he lived an isolated and solitary childhood. The Abbey was his playground. In its hallowed gloom and ancient splendour, the statues and tombstones were his companions.

'My father had the keys to various bits of the Abbey, so feeling terribly privileged I could explore everywhere. I could get out on to the roof at all sorts of different levels, and creep along the ledges inside and out.

'At night it was lovely. I would take my gramophone and play Handel

Dean's Yard, Westminster: playing among the sarcophagi and marble effigies

in the organ loft, immensely loud, and it sounded absolutely splendid, reverberating round the Abbey.

'Music was very important to me. I got to know a lot of choral music at the Abbey, hearing the St Matthew Passion every year, and attending all the carol services. Our family would sit in the stalls for the clergy, by the choir, and sing lustily.

'One big event of my boyhood was coming up from Winchester for the Coronation of George VI, when I had to wear hired Court dress from Moss Bros, black velvet breeches and a sword. My father had to carry one of the crowns at the ceremony, and apparently it was mislaid, and found again at the last minute.'

But on more ordinary days he wandered quite happily among the sarcophagi and obelisks, the marble effigies and the death-masks. Wasn't he alarmed by some of them? 'My favourite,' he said, 'is the skeleton tombstone, which used to alarm me terribly, like something out of an M. R. James story.'

It is the famous monument of Joseph Gascoigne Nightingale, one of

138

Roubiliac's best-known works. Mr Nightingale was walking on his terrace with his young wife, in 1731, when a flash of lightning gave her such a shock that she died; the monument shows Mr Nightingale holding his wife and trying to ward off Death in the form of a skeleton brandishing a spear.

It is hideously realistic and impressed the young Anthony hugely. John Wesley agreed: he thought the statue incomparable. 'Here, indeed, the marble seems to speak,' he said.

Dr Storr's favourite chapel was that of Henry VII, where the Knights of the Bath have their ceremonies, gaudy with the knights' banners and superbly roofed with fan-vaulting and hanging stone pendants. 'My brother was married in here,' recalls Dr Storr, 'and a few days before the ceremony one of those great stone corbels fell from the ceiling and made a huge dent in the marble floor. Had it happened days later it would have killed the best man. Repairing it meant re-doing the tracery of the whole roof – extremely expensive and difficult technically.'

The stalls of this chapel have some bizarre, carved misericords: monkeys, unicorns, monsters, mermaids, wife beating husband, David and Goliath. 'I was fascinated by these narrow seats,' said Dr Storr. 'They are hinged so that if the monks fell asleep and slumped forward, they would tip up and crash to the floor. I thought this was so cruel and so hard on them.'

Walking through the Abbey, which he had not done for so many years, Dr Storr reflected that it all looked very much cleaner and more brightly painted than in his boyhood. 'There was some feeling when it was all done up, that it looked too garish, that even in its original state the colours weren't so brilliant. The whole place really is a vast museum.'

The actual Abbey museum, of course, is in the Norman undercroft, full of dramatic waxen images of kings and heroes. For Anthony Storr it is the place where he slept in 1940, when he was on fire-watching duty.

The walls of Westminster School, in Little Dean's Yard, are remembered for their convenient blankness, so useful for knocking tennis-balls against; the Abbey garden, exquisitely carpeted with pink blossom that swirls about us like snowflakes, was where Nanny Guest (who came as a temp and stayed twenty years) would first wheel her young charge.

A walk through the thirteenth-century cloisters reveals that every stone is familiar. He remembers which bits were bombed and restored, and stops every few yards at a remembered memorial tablet underfoot. Having walked over Vaughan Williams and Elgar and Aphra Behn and Henry Purcell, we come to his own father's stone in the cloisters, Vernon Faithfull Storr: 'He helped many by his teaching and his example.'

139

'My father had been a don at Oxford originally and he suffered agonies of doubt about going into the Church. In about 1900 he gave a series of lectures trying to reconcile Darwinism with orthodox Christian belief. He was a learned man, an intellectual who always refused preferment.

'He refused two bishoprics; he was very insecure socially, having been brought up in extreme genteel poverty. He used to say he couldn't face all that entertaining. He hated social occasions, and never lost that, in spite of having to deal with Royalty and having considerable advisory power in the Church. He used to fuss my wretched mother dreadfully if she had people to dinner, always worrying that things wouldn't go right.

'He and my mother were first cousins; she was a Storr, too. She was an extremely self-sacrificing woman whom people often referred to as a saint. The worst thing I ever heard her say about anybody was, "I'm sure there must be something nice about him."

'In our house there was a perpetual atmosphere of over-anxiety about money. It was such an enormous house to keep up, and I was brought up to do all forms of housework, mopping and dusting and carpet-sweeping, to keep up standards, even though we had a cook and maids, all of whom were miserably underpaid.

'My father was a good writer too, so he wrote on religion for *The Times*, and did sermon notes for the Church of England newspaper, to save others the bother. He used to say that at least he would have given me a good education; but in fact he died during my first term at Cambridge, leaving nothing, and his friends got together enough money to get me through university, for which I am eternally grateful.'

No 20 Dean's Yard is the house. It is on the oldest, eastern side of the square, and the most interesting: faced by the duller nineteenth century buildings opposite. The vaulted ground floor dates from the fourteenth century, and with its triple-arched windows and ivy on the blackened walls, it blends with the Abbey better than any of the rest of the square.

Grass is now growing through the cracks in the doorstep; it turned out the house has not been lived in for about twenty years, and it has been declared unsafe.

A planning application emblazoned on the drainpipe informs us it is to be converted to house the administration department of the Abbey, and to form two flats.

Dr Storr hopes that the lower part of the house will be left alone. 'In the first floor there are some extraordinary Italian panelled frescoes, white on black plaster, of mythological figures, mermaids and seahorses, that were said to have been done by a pupil of Pietro Torrigiani, the craftsman who came over to do Henry VII's tomb.' Torrigiani is also well known as the rowdy youth who knocked his fellow pupil Michelangelo's nose in.

'On the ground floor was our dining-room, so we always had people peering in through the windows just as we are doing now.' It is hard to see much, except the distant prospect of more pretty arched windows at the back of the house.

'In this room we had our family prayers every morning. We were very much still living in a nineteenth century atmosphere. We were frightfully old-fashioned, and didn't have a telephone or a wireless or a car.

'We were such churchmice, we saved on everything. We saved on electric light by having little oil lamps on the stairs, really pinching. I was so rigidly brought up about electricity that I still fuss like mad about lights left on. The whole house was freezing too. I've never lived anywhere that was so perishingly, cold, we had *chilblains*. All the bedrooms were totally unheated; we huddled over the one coal fire.'

It was a case of sacrificing creature comforts for the aesthetic joy of the house and the loveliness of its situation. Robert Mayer concerts just over the road in the Central Hall; idyllic walks with father to St James' Park and over Westminster Bridge; the bustle of Strutton Ground market.

'On hot summer nights I would be allowed to sleep in a camp bed on the lead roof outside the nursery, facing the tower of the Abbey and with Big Ben booming out into the night. And, for a child, the house was full of secrets. A dark passage led straight into the Abbey cloisters, and a trapdoor led to an underground secret passage through to the next house, and the service lift down to the kitchen was big enough for a child to ride in.

'I really loved that house. I hated leaving it. It was so romantic and thrilling – the most incredible place to grow up in.'

CHAPTER TWENTY-SEVEN

Edith Palmer
Mayfair

It hardly took a moment to go back with Miss Edith Palmer to where she was young.

She was born in the very flat where I met her, in the next room to her living-room, eighty years ago this spring. It is in Balderton Street, right opposite Selfridges in Oxford Street. And she arrived there a good fifteen years before Selfridges did.

Miss Palmer was a florist. She worked where she lived, in smartest Mayfair. 'It was a dream, the Ritz ballroom,' she says. 'We could cover the stage in climbing green smilax with pips of rosebuds, and festoon the colonnades with rambling roses.'

Her Mayfair is another land and time, but however it may have changed it has never lost its elegance. It is utterly home ground to her, since she never ventured far from home: she worked for many years at Selfridges, in the flower and fruit halls, and at Peter Robinson's, and even for fifteen years at Keysign House, which is directly across the street from her flat. Commuting without tears.

'My great grandmother was born in the village of Kensington,' says Miss Palmer, 'and so was my grandmother and so was my mother.

'At sixteen my father came to live just round the corner from here, above his uncle's fruit shop, Palmer's, in North Audley Street. And when his uncle died he took over the shop. My mother and father were married at St Mark's, North Audley Street, and went just across the road for the reception.'

There is a picture in her priceless family album, of mother and father on honeymoon at Ramsgate: mother dark-eyed, solemn, with flowers in her hat; father equally solemn in a bowler. 'Isn't he a handsome bloke?' she says. 'Over six feet tall, and died at thirty-six. Of hard work I should think.'

She and her three brothers, all three born within yards of the flat she still lives in, were christened at St Mark's and went to the church school which is still derelict, a few feet from Miss Palmer's kitchen door. All three brothers died in the First World War.

'Harry was killed in Arras – I remember it was just after my twenty-first birthday. I was working in Selfridges' fruit department when the manageress came and told me the news. Then Charlie developed malignant malaria in Salonika, and then Ernie, the youngest, who was clerk to the Chief of Staff at the War Office, died after a breakdown: really he died of war service.'

Left with her widowed mother, Miss Palmer never thought of leaving home. She did spend one year as resident florist at the Waldorf, but went back home. She supposes she must have had offers of marriage – she was a beauty, certainly – but she says: 'After the war, all the boys and young men of my age were literally wiped out. You'd always be saying, "How's so and so?" to be told, "He's gone, gone."'

'Visualize my life. I would get up at four to be at the market at five with the van. We had two hours off in the afternoon and I was there till the shop closed, darn long hours. When I got home I stayed with my mother, and so the years rolled on.

'Our journeys were restricted, you don't realize with the freedom you have now,' she says. 'My brother Harry was engaged to a girl for three years and still her father wouldn't allow her out after nine o'clock.'

Still, she remembers jolly times. At Selfridges and at Keysign House she was always secretary of the sports and social clubs, organizing whist drives, dances and football teams, and playing a lot of tennis. A portrait on her wall shows her dressed up as Dick Turpin, very dashing, at one of her own fancy-dress balls.

And she belonged to Selfridges dramatic society, performing in *The Shop Girl* and *La Cigale* at the King's Theatre, Hammersmith. 'And after each show,' she says, 'Gordon Selfridge himself would entertain us to supper at the Savoy.'

Selfridges with its heavily-scented spectacular glamour, came along in 1909 – 'and without exaggeration, they used to have the prettiest shop-girls in London,' says Miss Palmer.

'Naturally, the girls today cannot compete.'

Before Selfridges arrived Miss Palmer remembers Oxford Street (formerly Tyburn Road, in the days of the gibbets) as an ordinary high street, not a particularly busy thoroughfare.

143

Selfridges from Balderton Street:
'They used to have the prettiest shop-girls in London'

On the site of Keysign House there was Thrupp and Maberley, the coachbuilders and repairers. 'So there was a line of stables opposite our flat, and always coaches waiting for repair.' Later Thrupp and Maberley gave way to Selfridges' food hall.

'On the corner of our street, where the Midland is now, there was a penny bank for small investors. I have a faint memory,' she adds, 'of crossing Oxford Street with my father, ducking underneath the horses' heads.'

Miss Palmer, in one of her many hats, was absolutely definite about which of her favourite walks we would take around Mayfair. 'We're coming into another world now,' she announced proudly. 'I want to show you a cottage from 1723, and the largest china shop in the world, and the smallest square. How about that?'

At the bottom of Balderton Street, on Brown Hart Gardens, is a romantic-looking oddity that turns out to be a power station. 'It used to be a garden, with a keeper and hut, provided by the first Duke of Westminster,' said Miss Palmer. 'When they built the power station they stipulated they must retain the garden for the tenants. So they put in what was termed an Italian garden, and there used to be goldfish, and seats all round. Since the war it's been neglected to my mind.'

144

We walked through the courtyards of the former stables, Providence Court and St George's Yard, into North Audley Street.

When Miss Palmer was fifteen she won a trade scholarship. 'But I didn't want my mother, who had brought up four children since 1900 without any assistance, to have the expense.

'So I walked round to a shop called Solomon's in North Audley Street and got myself apprenticed as a florist.' Solomon's is now a wine shop, Sado and King. Just beyond is peaceful Lees Place, where Mayfair Cottage stands, Miss Palmer's favourite house in the locality, built 1723 and fashionably restored in 1970.

The way to Grosvenor Square took us through Shepherd's Place, where the shops are all boarded up for redevelopment. F. White, stationer, established fifty years, has a notice: 'We regret very much that after all these years we shall be unable to serve you after 31 December 1973.'

Into Grosvenor Square, and 'that monstrosity!' as she calls the fine spread-eagled American Embassy. 'But if you'd only known,' she said, 'the beautiful private houses that were there before. Oh, it was a treat in the Season, to go round the houses when they were having their receptions, and do their flowers.'

Past the Connaught Hotel 'which used to be called the Coburg, but being a German name they altered it in the war'; and the neo-Gothic Jesuit Church in Farm Street, into the tombstone-ringed gardens of St George's, Hanover Square, which are overlooked by Miss Palmer's handsome old school, St George's.

Built in 1898, it is now a primary school, and as we walked through the gardens, Miss Palmer was gratified to mention that this Christmas some children from there brought her a bag of groceries. She told them she was a former pupil.

The front of the school is in South Street, where Florence Nightingale lived, and where Miss Palmer's favourite emporium stands on the corner of South Audley Street. It is Thomas Goode (established 1827) with its 'finest collection of china and crystal anywhere in the world today'.

We discovered Audley Square, her 'smallest square' which is now only half a square owing to the big brash Audley Square Garage and car park. 'I can't express my feelings about this,' said Miss Palmer, 'talking to a lady.'

And of course, Miss Palmer points out, Mayfair was a rather *risqué* area. 'In old days it was much more open. These women used to parade on the balconies in Regent Street, and I've heard men in the old days say they wouldn't dream of walking down Bond Street.'

Strange, this *mélange* of the scurrilous and the chic in Mayfair. Miss

145

Palmer as a girl would never walk out without spotless white gloves. 'I was always very susceptible to atmospheres,' Miss Palmer said. 'And I've never wanted to live in any other part of London. When I went to business it was so convenient, and what's more it's such a *nice* neighbourhood. You can't blame me for not wanting to move from where I am, can you?'

CHAPTER TWENTY-EIGHT

Douglas Jay
Woolwich

I wonder if suburb-dwellers ever try to imagine what came before their Mon Repos, before the green acres round London were enveloped in the mammoth suburban building sprawl between the wars. What, for instance, was the little arc of typical semis known now as Brinklow Crescent, SE18?

The people at No 72 Brinklow Crescent may like to know that they inhabit what was once Douglas Jay's artichoke patch.

Douglas Jay, Labour MP for North Battersea, spent a blissful early childhood in a grand Victorian house called Tower House, on the crest of Shooter's Hill. Now the house is gone, and its six acres of garden are carved into many quiet roads of archetypal villas like Brinklow Crescent.

Mr Jay, a gaunt figure in a black overcoat, strides these slopes with the proprietorial air of one whose land once stretched as far as the eye could see. He is quite certain about the artichoke patch.

'I was passionately devoted to the garden. In 1914 our younger gardener went off to the war, and in 1916 when they were taking even the lame, our very infirm old gardener went to the war, so at the age of nine I had to take it over. I truly loved the flowers. I was an absurdly romantic gardener and had secrets in every corner. Just *here*, there was a forest of artichokes six or seven feet high and we could make a path through to a hideaway in the middle.'

The way to Shooter's Hill is, Douglas Jay assures me, an historic route, being the old Roman Road and having associations with Wat Tyler.

Up Blackheath Hill we go, over the Common above Greenwich Park, where Douglas Jay remembers being taken to the Observatory on 11 August 1911, 'which I believe was the only day this century when the temperature reached a hundred degrees. The King was at Sandringham

Tower House, Shooter's Hill: 'secrets in every corner'

and Asquith was in the South of France, which just shows you how different things were.'

We approach Shooter's Hill, typical Roman road of resolute straightness (it's part of Watling Street, leading to Dover) via a broad thoroughfare lined with solid burghers' villas, where the Jays used to visit Dr McKearn, or more often have him visit them, in one of the first motor cars.

Past two famous military hospitals, the Brook and the Royal Herbert, which even now fill Douglas Jay with horror: 'By 1915 the whole neighbourhood of Shooter's Hill was packed with wounded soldiers, who all wore blue. My mother took on the job of visiting them and all through the summer we had them in our garden. I feel uneasy about hospitals even today.'

Opposite the turning into Shrewsbury Lane at the wood's edge stands the house where Sir Frederick Donaldson lived: 'He was superintendent of the Arsenal in the Great War. And was sunk in the *Hampshire*, along with Kitchener. Drowned.

'Of course the Arsenal, started by Queen Elizabeth, was the life of the whole of Woolwich.

'Funnily enough, my father took me round the Arsenal in 1916 when he was recruiting labour; and in the Second World War it was my job to recruit labour for the Arsenal.

'Now, of course, it's just a football team.'

Shrewsbury Lane was a quiet avenue of large houses behind trees, the first walk (in perambulator) that Douglas Jay remembers. 'Snobbish people

148

called it Shrowsbury, of course. At an early age I disapproved and called it Shrewsbury, because my nurse called it that, and that was good enough for me.'

We stop to gaze upon the fire station that caused a great thrill for the Jay children when it was built right opposite their gates in 1912, and opened by J. B. P. Kerslake, chairman of the LCC Fire Brigade Committee, as the plaque records. 'London's noble fire brigade,' quotes Douglas Jay from Hilaire Belloc's *Matilda*.

Right opposite is the top end of the Jays' garden: a curious mound, a grassy hump surrounded by railings and with a few beech trees on it. 'It's supposed to be a tumulus, an ancient neolithic burial-ground or something. Although it was in our garden it was protected by railings even then but my father had a key and we could get inside. We made a sandpit at one side, and dug a cave in the sand *just here*.'

There is nearby a water-tower on the brow of the hill. Mr Jay claims this can be seen from Hampstead. 'Whitestone Pond and Shooter's Hill are on the same elevation of about four hundred feet to the north and south of the Thames. It was the great schoolboy project to walk through the night from one to the other. But I'm afraid I never did it because I didn't at that time have the firmness of purpose.'

The hill of Brinklow Crescent ('our herbaceous borders') is quite steep. 'My father would walk right up here from Woolwich Arsenal station when he was on the LCC and took the puffer train home every night.' His reward was a sensational view.

Even in icy mist you could see the extent of the panorama, not just over all Woolwich but across dockland and the river. On golden days they would watch the ships up and down Galleons Reach; on this day only the tower blocks stood out against the gloom.

We can, however, make out the crossing of the Woolwich Free Ferry (still running, still free) across to Poplar and Silvertown, used constantly by Jay père. 'I remember the Silvertown Explosion of 1916,' says Mr Jay. 'An explosives factory blew up on the north side of the river, and all the glass from all the windows from Woolwich to New Cross was blown out. I was in our drawing-room and the curtains flew right up in the air and I was blown up off the sofa. The fire burned for six days.'

Called Tower House, the house had a big square tower sixty-four feet high, with the flag of St George flying from the top. 'The rooms in the tower were a sort of museum for my father's geological specimens. On a clear day you could see Hampstead and Highgate. And father had a telescope – typical Victorian obsession with scientific instruments – and all our guests would be taken up to the tower for that view.

149

'From the tower I watched a Zeppelin being brought down in flames at Potters Bar: there was a great roar of cheers from the street. It was treated like a football match and Plum Lane became a sort of grandstand for the Zeppelin raids.

'How very different from the Second World War. I came back here in 1940 to rescue my mother's former housekeeper who was hiding from the bombs crouched beneath the kitchen table.'

The garden covered six acres. There was a tennis court and a cricket pitch, a gardener's lodge, a large greenhouse with vines, and two fields with two fine Jersey cows because Mrs Jay believed that only fresh Jersey milk was suitable for children.

'There was a dahlia bed solely for picking, as well as one for looking at – an area bigger than my whole garden now. There were poplars and monkey puzzles and chestnut trees and fruit trees. These lime trees [on the pavement of Brinklow Crescent] formed an avenue down the garden. Strange to see the trees survive where nothing else has.'

To see the full view we climb towards Shrewsbury Park, a pleasant open space overlooking allotments. 'These allotments were started in the First World War: part of Lloyd George's campaign for growing our own food. Just down the hill, exactly where that dog is, was the point where I first asked my nurse why the schoolchildren I saw going in to Plum Lane School were barefooted. Why were they poor? I asked. And it was beyond my nurse's power to explain. So I resolved to find out.'

His father was a non-practising barrister who had inherited the great house 'from a relative, an old boy named Lord Teynham, Victorian eccentric.

'My father and mother were wholly devoted to good works.

'My father ran charities in the East End, organized charity before the days of old-age pensions and unemployment benefit. I suppose he was nominally a Tory, but through his East End work he got to know all the early Labour leaders, Will Thorne, Will Crooks, George Lansbury.

'My mother' (in photographs a pretty brown-eyed creature in Edwardian sleeves and straw boater, always nursing a dog or cat on her lap) 'ran guilds and clubs for her church. So the garden was always overrun by kids. I remember going to sleep to the sound of bats hitting balls.

'They both disliked the officers from the Royal Military Academy, known as the Shop, nearby. Woolwich was a strange society: there was us on top of the hill, you see, and there were the wage-earners on thirty shillings a week below. My parents were real Victorian Christians who believed in helping the weak and the needy, and the officers were snobbish and narrow-minded to a degree.

150

'We really grew up almost entirely with the working people from down the hill. Until an officer called Captain Passmore was billeted on us, and he was rather jolly.

'The British Army was something in those days. General Gordon and the British Grenadiers and brass bands. We would go on Sunday mornings and see the parades and the march past.

'So when I took *The Times* into my father that morning, with the news that war had been declared at nine o'clock last night I had a vision of soldiers in my mind.

'Father was ruined by the War. Income tax went up from a shilling to four and six in the pound. We sold the lease on the house to a Captain Fitzroy who must have later sold it to the property company who pulled it down and built these roads.

'When we moved to Hampstead in 1917 to escape the bombs, it was a drawing in of belts. Before 1914 we had had ten domestics, and we took only two. When my mother showed me the new house in East Heath Road – near the road she was born in, overlooking the Heath which was supposed to replace our lovely garden – I thought it was so small we should never be able to live there. It's now divided into five flats and the garden is a car park for twenty cars.'

Since then, except for the briefest of interludes. Douglas Jay has always lived in Hampstead. 'But at that time, as a boy of ten, it seemed a cruel blow to leave my house and my beloved garden. Leaving that was like leaving everything I had ever cared about.'

But Shooter's Hill has largely withstood urban sprawl, still verdant and wooded. Douglas Jay takes me to a fence where, at that time, London ended and meadow began. 'Beyond this, there were only the green fields of Kent. I'm glad they've preserved this meadow. To me, from here on seemed to be the distant country, remote and romantic.'

CHAPTER TWENTY-NINE

Jessie Matthews
Soho

Outside the Blue Posts pub in Berwick Street, Soho, there is a fruit and vegetable stall – the first of a line in the famous Berwick Street market. Jessie Matthews stood there one day smiling for the photographer, picking up apples and pears. 'Look, there's Jessie Matthews,' said passers-by. 'Doesn't she look well?'

Jessie Matthews, now in her sixties and positively blooming, is probably most latterly familiar to everyone as the last Mrs Dale, epitome of cosy middle-class respectability, a part she played to the manner born.

But sixty years ago, when her father had that very fruit stall outside the Blue Posts, Jessie Matthews was even better known in the market as the skinny little girl who ran everywhere. So full of energy was she, always skipping and dancing, that her mother took her to the clinic suspecting she was suffering from St Vitus' Dance.

It was in an upstairs room of the Blue Posts, which still has the bare boards and the piano in the corner, that nine-year-old Jessie Matthews first auditioned for the dancing teacher Elise Clare, who had once understudied Adeline Genée.

'She sat just there, by the window. And one of the little girls did a fouetté, and my sister Rosie called out: "My sister can do that – better!" I'd never done a fouetté in my life! It was the first time I'd seen one. But I did it, because Rosie had said that I could and I must.'

Rosie, eleven years older than Jessie, was more than a mother figure: she was coach, guide and chaperone. Their mother, working on the stall and always pregnant, must have been far too busy (after having fourteen children she then had twins) to be the mentor that Rosie was to Jessie. Convinced that her sister could be a dancing star, she positively made her one.

The house where Jessie Matthews was actually born was in the heart of the market at 94 Berwick Street, above a butcher's called J. Jacobson. It is still a butcher and now, by sheer coincidence, it is called Matthews.

The family moved out to Camden Town shortly, but then when Jessie was seven they moved back to Soho so that Dad could be nearer to his market-stall. They moved to just round the corner, a place above a stables called William and Mary Yard. It is now the site of an enormous garage.

Miss Matthews remembers being bitterly disappointed with the dinginess and slumminess of William and Mary Yard, and the gutters of Berwick Market piled with rotting vegetables. But she soon began to thrive on the Soho atmosphere: barrel-organs, bright lights, Piccadilly just round the corner, narrow streets, friendly people.

Now she realizes it was lucky to live there. 'It was a struggle, because we were so crowded and so poor. But it was marvellous from a career point of view. So convenient. Great. At the top of Windmill Street it was in the heart of the West End, for auditions and getting to the theatre. But although we just lived round the corner from everything I was always late. I would dash in five minutes late and join the end of the chorus line.

'Until one day André Charlot summoned me and told me he was taking me out of the chorus line. "Eet ees your own fault," he said, "for being so late." And then, he gave me my first small part in the show. That was his little joke. But he added, "Now you have responsibility you must learn not to be late again." And I never was. You can ask anyone in the profession. They'll tell you: Jessie Matthews is never late.'

Despite the constant childbearing, Mrs Matthews remains in Jessie's memory the picture of a woman who carried herself well: light of step, her well-shaped head held high, sitting in a ladder-back chair with always a baby in her lap. Though she had sixteen children only eleven survived. 'And her heart was big enough not only for all her children but for tramps and down-and-outs as well. We'd all be sitting at the long refectory table at William and Mary Yard and suddenly you'd look up and see a tramp, and be told, "Stop gawping."

'My father had a different kind of generosity. He was Mr What-You-Gonna-Have? He was surrounded by hangers-on, not friends really, and all the money he made in the market – £40 a week sometimes at Christmas, a lot of money then – would go in the pub. I've got an aversion to public houses ever since. And to people who take too much drink.

'I was the one who was sent along to the pub to bring him home, and I had to take his shoes off, take his muffler off, and I'd sing "I've got your shoe! I've got your sock!" to put him in a good humour. It's not much fun for a kid of ten or eleven, but I was the one who could get him into a good mood when he came home drunk.

Berwick Street market: 'the friendliest place to grow up in'

'But my mother never scolded him: she knew he'd never really grown up because he never had a proper childhood. His mother had abandoned him as a small baby, and he grew up tough as they come, fighting for his existence from the age of nine. Throughout my childhood I was frightened of my father.'

The stable yard housed three families: the Matthews, the Phillips with seven children, and the Dawsons with three. 'The Yard was a wonderful playground for the twenty or so children who lived there. We were always in and out of each other's houses. I used to like going to the Phillips, who were Jewish, where there'd be a pot bubbling on the stove: chicken soup and noodles. It seemed to me a luxurious place compared to our bare boards and windows without curtains.

'Mr Dawson was stage-manager at the Palladium, so whenever there was an animal act on at the Palladium, the animals would be housed in the

154

Yard and my Dad would look after them. He seemed to prefer animals to human beings.

'In the sheds and stables all the paraphernalia of the market was kept: the stalls, and vans, and the horses that pulled the carts from Covent Garden. There were ladders and packing cases, stable boys to play with, and of course the dogs and cats, a goat, rabbits and chickens.

'It was the friendliest possible place to grow up in, everyone being so kindly, looking after each other and sharing food. And those people have all bettered themselves I'm glad to say. They've all become successful people. Whenever I see them they are beautifully gowned and jewelled.'

It was in William and Mary Yard that Jessie first tried on a pair of ballet shoes: the neighbours' daughter had been given them by her boyfriend, lovely pink satin slippers from just near by at Gamba, the theatrical shoe shop in Old Compton Street. To Jessie they seemed the most desirable things in the world.

And to everyone's astonishment, when she slipped them on she tripped across the room on her points. 'A real dancer's foot,' the boyfriend said. That night the decisive Rosie announced to the family that Jessie was to be a dancer; and when she got her first wage-packet, from making button-holes at a Brewer Street shop, she bought Jessie her first practice shoes. Later it was Rosie who joined an elocution and drama class in Argyle Street and passed all she learned on to Jessie.

Jessie went to school at the old School Board of London's Pulteney Schools, tucked away in a surprisingly quiet corner of Peter Street, behind the Berwick Market. It forms one of those unexpected quarters that raffish, sleazy, noisy, anomalous Soho so often astonishes us with.

The school building, vintage 1880, is ivy covered, next door to a spec-tacular town garden of evergreens and half-hidden statuary, with a sunny yard in front of the entrance. The school is now part of Westminster College.

Jessie Matthews pauses on the stairs to point out where she used to change into her best dancing clothes to nip straight out of school to per-form at a charity concert at some hospital – Rosie standing by, urging her to get away early by pretending to be ill. 'I pretended to be ill so often, I actually did make myself sick,' says Jessie, 'worrying about telling lies.'

And upstairs is the place where her mother, enraged to be told by Jessie that her teacher had accused her of having dirty knickers, marched along to the class and stripped Jessie down to her petticoat and liberty bodice in front of her friends, to display the whiteness of her underwear. 'We may be poor but we're not dirty,' she declared.

Up on the roof was the only place for a play-yard in crowded Soho. Here

Jessie would stand at break and wave to her mother across the rooftops in William and Mary Yard. Today it is impossible to see so far, for the tall blocks of flats and offices that have sprung up all around the school.

By the age of eleven she was 'Little Jessie Matthews' billed as principal child dancer in *Dick Whittington* at the Kennington Theatre – an achievement that was somewhat dampened when a new girl came along and was given that role instead. The girl was Alice Marks, aged ten; later Alicia Markova.

She was 'Jessie Matthews, your favourite dancer' soon; playing *Red Riding Hood* at the Kilburn Empire, *Babes in the Wood* at the Alexandra Theatre in Stoke Newington; playing the Old Met, the Metropolitan in the Edgware Road. At school, she says, she became a proper little show-off. At home she didn't have to do housework, to keep her hands white, and she didn't have to help out on the market-stall. No wonder three of her sisters got the idea and became dancers too – Carrie, Lena and Eve.

She wanted the family to better themselves, and do well: she gave the Lord Chancellor, Lord Elwyn Jones, his first job when he came down from Cambridge, coaching her brother Eddie that he might go to college. She does a delightful impersonation of Eddie's Cockney accent. He did go to college, she says, but she can't recall where.

C. B. Cochran, one of whose Young Ladies she became along with Dame Anna Neagle, remembered in his own autobiography how the child Jessie looked to him when (of course) Rosie marched her to an audition. 'Jessie was an interesting looking child with big eyes, a funny little nose, clothes which seemed a bit too big for her and a huge umbrella. It may have been an ordinary-sized umbrella, but it seemed to dwarf her. "You're engaged, my dear," I said when she had finished her song and dance.'

So, it was America at fifteen, understudying Gertrude Lawrence; marriage at eighteen to Harry Lytton, son of Sir Henry Lytton of the D'Oyly Carte Opera Company, and a career as one of the first pin-ups and a fine actress. Rags, as they say, to riches.

'Oh yes, I was lucky to be born in Soho. Otherwise how would I have got on to the stage so quickly, how would all this have happened to me?' she says. 'Mind you, it wasn't what I wanted, really. It was Rosie who wanted it all for me, not me. It was Rosie who organized everything. She's nearly eighty now, and those black eyes of hers still flash.

'We came down to Berwick Market the other day together. She got herself behind a stall, just like in the old days, and twirled a bag of apples in her hands – and though she's quite frail now, she really came alive at that moment.'

CHAPTER THIRTY

Christopher Milne
Chelsea

Nobody grows up without having read *When We Were Very Young*, by A. A. Milne. Or at least *Winnie the Pooh* or *Now We Are Six*. And the hero of those books will always be childhood personified: Christopher Robin in his little checked smock, going upstairs with Pooh bumping at his heels, so perfectly drawn by Ernest Shepard.

The real Christopher Robin (now just Christopher if you please) has of course grown up like the rest of us – he is in his mid-fifties – and, diffident and gentle and rather shy, is very happy running a very popular bookshop in Dartmouth, Devon.

The only trouble is that people keep bringing in their children to shake hands with the real Christopher Robin.

When Christopher Robin Milne was very young, he would watch his father at the breakfast table opening letters. There were letters from students, wanting to know autobiographical details; there were letters from children, wanting autographs; there were begging letters too. A. A. Milne would pass the letters to his wife and ask what she thought.

'Probably Wol,' she would say. This was a reference to Owl's advice in Winnie the Pooh. Rabbit finds the notice saying GON OUT BACKSON BISY BACKSON, takes it round to Owl for advice, and Owl asks him what he did. 'Nothing,' says Rabbit. 'The best thing,' says Owl wisely. So the 'Wol' letters remained unanswered.

But now, these decades later, Christopher Robin has decided that it is time to write a reply to all those collective letters: so he has written a delightful book about his childhood called *The Enchanted Places*.

He was born in Mallord Street, Chelsea, at No 11 which is now re-numbered 13. A handsome house in the cottage style peculiar to Chelsea,

157

Mallord Street, where Christopher Robin was very young

prettily leaded windows with interesting upper bays, and tiny gardens front and back.

'The smell of the fuchsias and the colour of the geraniums is embedded for ever in my memory,' said Christopher Milne, finding the house much the same when we went back there together.

He led, as a small child, the kind of life children of his background were expected to lead: most of the time was spent in playing, eating, sleeping, in the nursery and night nursery on the top floor with Nannie.

He would be taken downstairs to visit parents three times a day: in the morning, while mother and father finished their breakfast; after tea, in the drawing-room, when he could play on the sofa or father's armchair and in the dining-room in the evening, where he could play 'boofy games' with mother, under the table in the dark.

Thirteen Mallord Street is now the home of Dr Kevin Connolly, his wife and two children. They knew of the Pooh connection when we called, because some years ago a film was made about Milne and Shepard and for some time there was an enormous Winnie in an upstairs window.

After the Milnes left the house, it was the home of Lord Fairfax of the Cameroons. The Connollys have made a neat white patio courtyard from

158

the tiny back garden that the Milnes barely used (they had their country acres at Cotchford). Upstairs is Christopher Robin's nursery where he said his prayers, and the bars on the windows to stop him falling out.

'I once threw my mother's wedding ring out of the window and down the drainpipe, just for something to do,' he says. 'Luckily my mother didn't like it much anyway. It was a big fat gold one and she then acquired a slim platinum one.'

Outside, Mallord Street was quiet, as it still is today.

'It was a quiet, almost deserted street, no cars, no people, no noise, nothing to look at,' says Christopher. But there were moments of liveliness that don't happen today when he would rush to the ottoman and clamber up to watch out of the window: a yodelling would herald the logman, with his horse and cart piled with logs; the ringing of a handbell preceded the muffin man, his tray of muffins on his head; there was the coalman pouring coal into the cellars, the organ-grinder, and the harp man, who came on Friday evenings and sat on a stool opposite Christopher's window.

'He had black hair, a small moustache, a dark grey coat and an air of quiet melancholy. I was allowed to go downstairs and cross the road: and I would put two pennies into his little velvet bag.'

Occasionally, Augustus John (who lived opposite) would stride by, beard and hair streaming.

Christopher Milne remembers his father as a mixture of opposites: 'Shy yet self-confident; modest, yet proud of what he had done; quiet, yet a good talker; warm, yet with a thin lip and ice cold eye that might, if you said the wrong thing, be pretty chilling; sympathetic, yet unsympathetic to what he felt was stupidity; friendly, yet picking his friends with care.'

The love and understanding of children that seems to pervade his books was not inordinate, nor sentimental. With his one and only son he seems to have been amiable, but distant. 'My father's heart remained buttoned up all through his life,' Christopher Milne says.

Mrs Milne seems to have been an ideal wife. She was a de Selincourt, as in Ernest de Selincourt the famous Wordsworth scholar.

'The de Selincourts were either very academic or very unacademic,' says Christopher Milne, 'just as Rabbit said to Owl: "You and I have brains. The others have fluff." My mother had fluff.' But her essential value to A. A. Milne is summed up by him in his autobiography: 'She laughed at my jokes.'

Christopher Milne says, quite rightly, that this was an absolutely vital qualification for his mother to have, and her sense of humour meant that all the things A. A. Milne liked but she didn't, like playing golf and watching cricket, didn't matter a bit. They laughed a lot together and were happy.

Christopher was an only child, but not a lonely child; Christopher Robin had a friend he still keeps in touch with, actually called Robin Hood, and he had a best friend called Anne.

> When Anne and I go out a walk
> We hold each other's hand and talk
> Of all the things we mean to do
> When Anne and I are forty-two

And it was true, the Milnes hoped to see Christopher Robin and Anne one day marry. Anne is now dead but she and Christopher's parents always remained friends.

Anne's family lived in Beaufort Mansions, half a mile away. Her 'Cooooo-eeee' would herald her arrival, and they two went everywhere together. They both went to a Miss Walters' kindergarten in Tite Street, leaving Pooh and Anne's monkey, Jumbo, behind; Christopher Milne will point out the exact place where one morning Anne told him that Father Christmas didn't exist.

Sometimes he and Anne went with their nannies to the Albert Memorial, sometimes to the Embankment Gardens or across the Albert Bridge to Battersea Park, taking hoops or skipping-ropes. But though this all makes him sound exactly like the little boy in the A. A. Milne books, Christopher Milne says sometimes he was and sometimes he wasn't.

'At The Zoo, for example, is about me. The Engineer is not.'

He certainly used to go and watch the changing of the guard at Buckingham Palace but he absolutely *insists* that his nannie would never have said, dismissingly, 'Sure to dear, but it's time for tea.' *His* nannie always had time to answer questions properly, put his mind at ease, do what he asked.

When he went off to boarding-school, nannie married Alfred who had waited all those years for her, and they lived in a bungalow which they called Vespers, after the 'Christopher Robin is saying his prayers' poem.

He was small, shy, and unselfpossessed, he says, not very bright at school (though he did go on to Cambridge) but good with his hands. By the age of seven he was the family's Chief Mender of Things. He liked sewing and knitting and making tapestry pictures, and he made a grandfather clock. It still rankles with him terribly that in The Engineer poem, about the train with a brake, his father had him say, 'It's a good sort of brake but it hasn't worked yet.'

'If I'd had a train – and I didn't have a train – any brake that I'd wanted to make for it – any simple thing like a brake – WOULD HAVE WORKED!' cries Christopher Milne.

160

What is peculiar about having had such a publicly lived childhood is that he still isn't quite sure of the distinction between the fact and the fiction.

'It is difficult to be sure which came first,' he writes in his book. 'Did I do something and did my father then write a story around it? Or was it the other way about, and did the story come first? . . . In the end it was all the same: the stories became part of our lives; we lived them, thought them, spoke them.'

He still isn't certain whether he or his father invented Pooh-sticks; but he is sure that *after* the story, when they were down at Cotchford Farm, they used to stand on Pooh-sticks bridge and throw the sticks into the water, living out the legend.

In his twenties Christopher took a flat at 67 Chancery Lane. It is an indelibly memorable address, because, as the Milnes discovered, it is mentioned in George Bernard Shaw's *Mrs Warren's Profession*. At the end of Act III, Frank says, 'Where are you going to? Where shall we find you?' and Zizie, Mrs Warren's daughter, replies: 'At Honoria Fraser Chambers, 67 Chancery Lane, for the rest of my life.' Shaw describes it as very modern (for 1894), with plate-glass windows, distempered walls, and electric light.

'My father wrote to Shaw to ask him why he had picked that particular address,' says Christopher Milne.

'And he sent a card back to explain that Eleanor Marx lived there, the daughter of Karl. The flat had been a sort of meeting-place for early feminists, who smoked cigarettes out of long holders.' In fact Zizie may have been based on Tussy Marx, since in the play she says she smokes cigarettes because men object to the smell of cigars.

During our day out we took a detour round to Miss Walters's school on the corner of Tite Street, to find that the building was empty, and the door bricked up; but the funniest thing was that somebody had chalked in very large letters on the wall: 'POOH'.

'Extraordinary,' said Christopher Milne. Perhaps it's true, even in 1974, that

> Wherever I go, there's always Pooh,
> There's always Pooh and Me.

Remember? 'Oh, Bear!' said Christopher Robin. 'How I do love you!' 'So do I,' said Pooh.